English for Academic Study

New edition

Listening

Course Book

Colin Campbell and Jonathan Smith

Credits

Published by

Garnet Publishing Ltd
8 Southern Court
South Street
Reading RG1 4QS, UK

This edition first published 2012

Reprinted 2013, 2014, 2015.

ISBN: 978 1 90861 433 9

British Library Cataloguing-in-Publication Data
A catalogue record for this book is available from the British Library.

Production

Project manager:	Fiona Dempsey
Project consultant:	Fiona McGarry
Editorial team:	Fiona Dempsey, Peter Finn
Art director:	Mike Hinks
Design and layout:	Simon Ellway, Maddy Lane, Ian Lansley
Photography:	Corbis, Alamy, iStock, Mott MacDonald Group Ltd
Audio:	Tom, Dick and Debbie Productions

Printed and bound in Lebanon by International Press: interpress@int-press.com

Acknowledgements

A large number of people contributed in different ways to the production of this book, although all responsibility for any mistakes remains ours alone.

We would like to thank the following for their permission to use extracts from the lectures that were originally recorded as part of the British Academic Spoken English (BASE) corpus:

Prof Michael Utton, Prof Alan Roberts (Rennes Business School, France), Dr Steve Wiggins, Alan Rowley, Dr Clare Furneaux, Dr Elizabeth Gaffan, Dr Colin Beardsley, Prof Peter Roach and Dr Rupert Loader.

In addition we would like to thank Shelagh Tonkyn for permission to use an extract from a lecture on magistrates' courts given at the University of Reading, and acknowledge the influence of the ideas of Beverly Fairfax on features of lecture introductions in Unit 2, and those of Tony Lynch on ideas on note-taking in Unit 4 of this book.

Our colleagues, Dr Paul Thompson and Sarah Creer, were very helpful in making the BASE corpus available and accessible to us, and in suggesting suitable lectures from the corpus.

The following colleagues gave invaluable feedback on parts of this book, and their contribution is gratefully acknowledged: Emma Grenside, Bruce Howell, Anne Pallant, John Slaght, Lucy Watson and Sebastian Watkins. We would also like to thank Nicola Taylor and her in-sessional students for giving us the opportunity to trial some of the material in the book.

Colin Campbell and Jonathan Smith, March 2012

c Contents

Book map

	Unit title and topics	Skills focus	Microskills
1	**Listening and lectures** *Problems of listening* *Differences between academic cultures*	■ Listening in different languages ■ Issues in understanding spoken English ■ Listening to lectures	
2	**Introductions to lectures** *Migration* *Britain and the European Monetary Union* *Globalization* *Magistrates' courts*	■ Thinking about introductions ■ Functions and language of lecture introductions ■ Listening to lecture introductions	■ Word stress
3	**Identifying key ideas in lectures** *Franchising*	■ Thinking about key ideas ■ Identifying key points in a lecture ■ Distinguishing key points from examples ■ Signposting and highlighting key points	■ Word families (1)
4	**Note-taking: Part 1** *Britain's traffic problems* *The East-Asian economic miracle*	■ Reasons for taking notes ■ Principles of note-taking ■ Note-taking practice	■ Sentence stress
5	**Note-taking: Part 2** *Language learning* *Changes in the world economy* *Health in the UK*	■ Returning to your notes ■ Using abbreviations and symbols ■ Organizing your notes	■ Word boundaries
6	**Introducing new terminology** *Embedded words* *European Union: regulations and directives* *Market dominance and monopoly*	■ Introducing new terminology ■ Introducing terms and concepts	■ Weak forms of function words
7	**What lecturers do in lectures** *Doing market research* *Social learning* *Contestable markets*	■ Macrostructure of lectures	■ Word families (2)
8	**Digressions** *Social learning* *Questionnaire design* *Integrated rural development*	■ Reasons for digressions ■ Identifying digressions	■ Common expressions in lectures

i Introduction

Aims of the course

The purpose of this book is to help you better understand spoken English, particularly the spoken English of academic lectures, as well as to help you develop your note-taking skills while listening.

Structure of the course

- **Unit structure:** Apart from the first unit, all the units are divided into two sections: **macroskills** and **microskills**.

Macroskills include such things as:
- making use of lecture introductions
- note-taking
- recognizing the structure of lectures

Microskills focus on understanding linguistic features of spoken English such as:
- recognizing words that are spoken quickly and are not stressed
- recognizing where one spoken word ends and the next begins
- word **stress** and sentence stress

In these units you will also find the following items:
- **Sound advice:** These either summarize key points from the unit or present advice on **listening strategies.**
- **Study tips:** These have been included for ease of reference when you are revising what you have studied. They either summarize the outcome of a series of activities or are a summary of other information contained in the unit.
- **Unit summaries:** Each unit is followed by a unit summary, giving you the opportunity to reflect on what you have learnt.

Additional materials

Glossary: Words or phrases in **bold** (or **bold** and <u>underlined</u> in task instructions) in the text are explained in the glossary on page 70.

Transcripts: At the end of the book you will find the transcripts of all the lectures. Your teacher will sometimes give you the opportunity to listen to the recordings and follow the transcript at the same time, once you have completed the main listening tasks.

Working with the course

It can be particularly challenging to listen to long stretches of speech in a foreign language, particularly when you are not aware of the general structure of academic lectures given in English. This book will provide you with:
- guided instruction on how to follow a lecture.
- the opportunity to practise listening to similar lectures to the ones you will meet in your future studies.

What you put into the course will determine how much you get out of it. Obviously, if you want to improve your skills in listening to lectures and taking notes, it is essential to practise this skill. You should therefore prepare well for the sessions, as well as participating actively in them.

Listening materials

Many of the lecture extracts in this book are based on transcripts of **authentic** lectures given at the University of Reading. These lectures were given to audiences of British and international students as part of their normal degree programmes. Although the extracts have been re-recorded to ensure clarity, the language and content of these lectures have been maintained, to ensure that you are provided with listening practice that closely simulates listening to, and note-taking from, real academic lectures.

The lecture extracts are taken from a range of academic fields, including investment banking, development economics, marketing, psychology and linguistics. Although the original lectures were intended for students doing degrees in these subjects, we have chosen extracts that should be accessible to students of all subjects.

Other extracts have been written specially for this book, but have been designed to reflect features of authentic academic lectures.

> The ▶ symbol indicates that the recordings are available on both audio CD and DVD.

Vocabulary

Although the recordings in the book may not be related to your particular subject, you will find a lot of useful vocabulary in this book.

There are different types of vocabulary that you may find useful:
- **Academic words:** These are words that occur frequently in many different academic subjects, so whatever your degree subject, it is important to learn how to use them.
- **Non-technical topic words:** Many of the recordings use sets of topic vocabulary which will be useful to students on almost all degree courses; for example, the text on market research contains many words connected with surveys, questionnaires and statistics.
- **Subject-specific words:** Some of the recordings contain words which will be of particular interest to students of specific subjects; for example, there is an extract on social learning which will be of particular interest to students planning to study psychology.

Listening outside the classroom

Your listening will improve more quickly if you practise outside the classroom. You can do this in a variety of ways; for example, talking with English-speaking friends, listening to the radio or watching TV, or working with independent study materials (see further below).

You will find *Sound advice* sections in most units in this book, and these contain useful advice for improving your listening. Here are some more ideas.
- There are a number of good websites which provide practice in listening to academic lectures. If you go to the EAS website (enter through **www.englishforacademicstudy.com**) you will find links to some of these sites.
- A wide range of vocabulary is part of the key to success in listening. You should keep a record of new words or phrases that you learn, and make sure you note down the pronunciation, particularly if it does not fit in with pronunciation patterns you are familiar with. Ask your teacher to model the pronunciation if you are not sure of it.
- There are several dictionaries on CD-ROM where you can hear the pronunciation and see the meaning of a word on screen, either by moving the mouse pointer over a word or by clicking on it. The *Macmillan English Dictionary* and *Longman Dictionary of Contemporary English* both have good CD-ROM versions. Think about buying one of these because it will be useful, not just on this course, but in your later studies.

Listening to longer talks, and talks about your own subject, will help prepare you for listening to lectures, so you will need to do more independent listening in your own time.

Additional audio-visual resources

To help improve your extended listening, you can access highly relevant lectures and talks on two websites – the University of Reading's SACLL site, and TED Talks.

Self-Access Centre for Language Learning website (University of Reading)

This has more than 30 lectures given to international students on pre-sessional courses at the university's International Study and Language Centre on academic and general topics; many of these are by distinguished lecturers in disciplines such as construction management, food science, investment, psychology, finance and management. Each lecture is 35–50 minutes long and comes with transcripts and tasks, both of which can help your listening.

Here is a guide to using the material effectively.
- Find the website by typing in the URL **www.sacll.co.uk** or entering 'SACLL lectures Reading' into Google or another search engine.
- Check through the lecture list, read the brief descriptions and choose one that interests you.
- Click the task button for your chosen lecture to get a list of open questions about the lecture.
- Read the questions and check any unknown vocabulary – reading and understanding the questions will help you anticipate the lecture's content.
- If necessary, do a quick Google search on the lecture topic to gain some more background knowledge. On degree courses, doing background reading before lectures is essential to full understanding.
- Listen to Part 1 of the lecture. Here, the speakers typically a) introduce the topic, b) say why it is important and c) explain how they will organize the lecture. Understanding this is essential to understanding the whole lecture (see Unit 2 on lecture introductions).
- As you listen to Part 1, answer the questions in the task.
- Check your answers to the questions on Part 1. If you have answered these correctly you will be well placed to understand the rest of the lecture. Otherwise, it is a good idea to listen again with the answers in front of you.
- Listen to the rest of the lecture. You could do this in parts, but it may be better to listen to the whole lecture without pausing, as you will need to develop the stamina needed for listening to long talks, rather than the shorter extracts that appear in this book.
- If you found parts of the lecture particularly hard to understand, or had problems answering the questions correctly, it is worth a) looking at the answers and listening again or b) reading the transcript while listening. This can help you understand why you have misheard or misunderstood.
- Spoken English can be harder to understand than written English, due to things like **word and sentence stress** (Units 2 and 4), **word boundaries** (Unit 5) and **weak forms** of words (Unit 6). One way to practise is to listen to a very short extract of a lecture, then try to write down exactly what the speaker says. Listen several times to do this. Then check the transcript and see if you have heard correctly. This may show you why you are having problems following spoken English.

TED Talks

Speakers on this interesting site include world-famous academics, writers, thinkers, medical researchers, politicians, investors, cooks, businesspeople and artists. The talks are informative, up to date and thought-provoking. They vary from three minutes to more than an hour in length. You will hear different accents that will help you prepare for study at a culturally diverse university.

Here are some suggestions on using this website effectively.
- The URL is **www.ted.com**, or just enter 'ted talks' into a search engine.
- You can access the talks in different ways. The top of the homepage has a menu including 'Themes', 'Speakers', 'Talks'. You can search for a particular speaker, e.g., Bill Gates, or the 'Themes' button may offer a more interesting way to access talks – giving you a choice of talks on related topics.

- Each screen has a thumbnail picture of the speaker next to the title of their talk. Click on a photo for a talk you think might be interesting.
- You will find brief information about the talk and the speaker accompanying the video.
- To find out more before you listen, try entering the speaker's name and some key words from the title into a search engine. Reading before attending lectures is key to successful understanding.
- TED Talks also provides transcripts of the talks, which you can keep open on-screen together with the video, plus translations and subtitles in various languages. However, for your first listening we recommend that you initially just listen to the introduction and perhaps pause to check the transcript, then open the transcripts or subtitles later.
- Listen to the rest of the lecture and make notes. If anything is unclear, listen again. If it is still unclear, look at that part of the transcript and listen again.
  Why did you not understand?
  Were there unknown words?
  Perhaps you did not recognize the pronunciation of a word you know in written form – remember, in connected speech, pronunciation can also be affected by the sounds in words before or after. Perhaps it was hard to recognize word boundaries (see Unit 5) – e.g., you might not hear the unstressed first **syllable** in *attempt* and hear 'tempt' instead. Perhaps you heard a word you knew but that seemed to have a different meaning, e.g., you might hear *fair* and recognize it as meaning 'light-coloured' (as in *fair hair*), but not know it can also mean 'just' (as in *justice*). Or, was the idea not clearly expressed or hard to understand even though you knew all the words? Understanding why you have had problems can help you listen more effectively next time.
- Finally, you may want to listen to the talk again, or part of it, with the transcript open, paying attention to the way words are pronounced in connected speech.

1 Listening and lectures

In this unit you will:

- discuss the different situations in which you have to listen
- identify what factors influence your ability to understand
- learn about features of lectures in different academic cultures

Task 1 Listening in different languages

1.1 **Discuss the following questions with another student.**

1. Which of these types of listening do you think is more difficult or requires more attention in your own language? Why?
   a. Listening to friends as part of your conversation with them.
   b. Listening to the radio.
   c. Listening to announcements at a crowded railway station.
   d. Listening to an academic lecture.
2. What experiences have you had of listening to spoken English?
3. What type of listening in English do you find more demanding/less demanding?

Task 2 Understanding spoken English

2.1 **Look at the following factors which make it difficult to listen to and understand spoken English. Add two or three more factors to this list and compare your ideas with your partner.**

- The speed at which someone is speaking.

- **Background noise.**

- _____

- _____

- _____

2.2 ▶ **CD1: 1** Listen to Part 1 of a talk in which a lecturer describes some of the problems of listening. Then answer the following questions.

1. Which of the factors listed in Ex 2.1 does she talk about?
2. Which other factors does she talk about?
3. After talking about the factors which affect listening, the lecturer discusses two additional problems that students may have. What are they?

2.3 ▶ **CD1: 2** Now listen to Part 2 of the talk. The lecturer asks you to write down a phrase. Do this as you listen.

_____

Does this example make the points in Ex 2.2 question 3 clearer?

2.4 ▶ **CD1: 3** Listen to Part 3 of the talk. Complete this <u>excerpt</u> by writing two to six words in each space.

So what is the solution to these two problems? Well, firstly, you need to get as much practice listening to natural speech as possible. Listen to _____ _____ and try to develop your understanding of how words and phrases are really pronounced, not how you _____ pronounced. And secondly, you need to accept that when you listen you may misunderstand what is being said. So you need to be ready to _____ _____ about your understanding of the meaning, if what you hear _____ compared to what you understood before. And this means taking a flexible, open-minded approach to listening.

2.5 Reflect on the talk you listened to in Ex 2.2–2.4. Answer the following questions.

1. Did you have any difficulties doing this activity?
2. If so, why do you think you had problems?
3. Were they the same problems the lecturer talked about?

Task 3 | Listening to lectures

You are going to listen to a lecturer talking about the differences he perceives between lectures in the UK and in China.

3.1 **Discuss with another student your experiences of lectures in your own country and/or in the country where you are studying. Think about:**
- what the lecturers did, e.g., read from notes, used visuals, asked questions, etc.
- what the students did, e.g., asked questions, took notes, etc.

3.2 ▶ **CD1: 4 In Part 1 of the talk, the lecturer describes the following:**
1. what his main interest is
2. where he got his information about lectures in China
3. the survey he did and the students he talked to

Listen to Part 1 of the talk and make notes about points 1–3.

3.3 **Compare your notes for Ex 3.2 with your partner. Then answer the following questions.**
1. Did you record the same information?
2. Could you have recorded the information in different ways using fewer words/different words? How?

3.4 ▶ **CD1: 5 In Part 2 of the talk, the lecturer first talks about some of the characteristics of lectures in China and then compares these with lectures in the UK. Listen and make notes on the main points he makes.**

China	UK

3.5 **Compare your notes for Ex 3.4 with your partner. Then answer the following questions.**

1. Did you record the same information?
2. Could you have recorded the information in different ways, using fewer words/ different words? How?

3.6 **Now respond to the talk. Look at the following questions in groups, and discuss your reactions to what the lecturer said in Ex 3.2 and 3.4.**

1. If you are from China, do you agree with what the speaker reported about lectures in China?
2. If you are from another country, are the lectures in your country more like the British system, the Chinese one, or a combination of both?
3. Have you listened to lectures in English before?
4. Did you take notes (in English or your own language) during the lectures you attended?
5. Was it difficult to take notes? If so, why?
6. What did you do before and after your lectures to help you understand more fully and remember the content?

Unit summary

You have discussed different situations in which you have to listen. You have identified factors that influence your ability to understand, and learnt about features of lectures in different academic cultures.

1 **Look at listening <u>issues</u> a–j and decide in which circumstances they could affect you. Choose one of the circumstances below and write F, L, R or A in the first box.**

F – This affects me when I speak to English-speaking friends.

L – This affects me when I listen to lectures.

R – This affects me when I listen to the radio or watch TV.

A – This affects me if I listen to announcements.

a. You are concentrating on something else at the same time as you are listening.

b. You are nervous because missing something important will have a negative consequence.

c. The speaker is using lots of words and phrases that you don't know.

d. The speaker talks very quickly and runs words together. Even common words are difficult to catch.

e. The speaker does not do or say things in the way that somebody in your country would.

f. The speaker is talking about a topic you know nothing about.

g. The speaker is using a lot of specialized vocabulary.

h. Other people interrupt the speaker so you can't follow the flow.

i. The speaker doesn't tell you when you should listen especially carefully.

j. There is a lot of background noise.

2 **Now look again at each issue and decide whether it is a problem for you or not. In the second box, write P if it is a problem and you need to practise, or N if it is not a problem.**

3 **Which of these issues did the lecturer in this unit offer solutions to?**

For web resources relevant to this book, see:
www.englishforacademicstudy.com

These weblinks will provide you with further practice in listening to lectures and information about issues concerning cultural differences.

2 Introductions to lectures

In this unit you will:

- look at how a lecture introduction can help you to understand the lecture better
- practise making notes on introductions to lectures
- learn how to recognize words that may be pronounced differently to the way you expect them to be

---

| Task 1 | **Thinking about introductions** |

1.1   **What do you expect the lecturer to talk about in the introduction to a lecture?**

1.2   **Think of lectures you have heard. Did the lecturers try to make the structure of the lecture obvious to students? If so, how?**

1.3   **Two students took notes on the introduction to a lecture about migration. Look at the notes they took. How are the notes different?**

Student 1:

> Migration from new EU countries, e.g., Poland – effect on UK econ., etc.

Student 2:

> Not EU migration BUT internal UK migration, e.g., country ➜ city

1.4   ▶ **CD1: 6 Listen to the introduction. Then answer the questions.**

1. Which student understood what the lecturer was going to talk about?
2. Why do you think the other student made a mistake?
3. Which words in the introduction **signal** what the lecturer will talk about?

Sound advice:

In an introduction, the speaker may define the **scope** of the lecture by explaining what will *not* be discussed, as well as what *will* be discussed.

Task 2 — Functions and language of lecture introductions

The left-hand column shows what lecturers commonly do in introductions to lectures. All the statements in the right-hand column are examples from introductions to lectures.

2.1 **Read the functions 1–9 in the left-hand column of the table.**

a. Tick (✓) those you discussed in Ex 1.1 and 1.2. Check you understand what the others mean.

b. Match 1–9 from the left-hand column to the statements a–i in the right-hand column.

What lecturers do in introductions	Lecturer statements
1. ☐ **limit the scope of the lecture;** in other words, say what they will talk about and what they will not talk about	**a.** ☐ There are in a sense two themes – there's a qualitative stream of market research and there's a quantitative stream. I'm going to deal with basically the quantitative stream of data collection first.
2. ☐ **comment on a theory** they have just described	**b.** ☐ However, that's not the type of migration that I want to look at today. What I want to look at is internal migration, i.e., the movement of people from country to city, and vice versa, and from one city to another.
3. ☐ **preview the content or structure** of the current lecture	**c.** ☐ Sara Shettleworth has a superb chapter on social learning, and I'm going to mention just a few of the examples that she mentions.
4. ☐ **refer to research** on the subject – this often includes mentioning specific reading material	**d.** ☐ What I want to do first, because I know some of you are not from the EU, is just give a very simple introduction to European Union institutions.
5. ☐ **give background information** on the lecture topic	**e.** ☐ I undertook a study in the mid-80s and it was quite easy for me to find 22 markets.
6. ☐ **introduce different approaches** to the subject	**f.** ☐ I'll be giving you a handout with these quotes, so you don't have to write them down verbatim.
7. ☐ **refer** to what students should/ should not write down	**g.** ☐ My **critique** about the theory of perfect contestability is that if you change the assumptions slightly, the predictions change dramatically. It's very unstable.
8. ☐ **indicate that they are referring back** to previous lectures and remind students of the content of those lectures	**h.** ☐ Last term we looked at how accounting systems were different. We looked at France and Germany and the Netherlands, and so forth, to see how the financial reports are different.
9. ☐ **explain the lecturer's own interest** in the subject, for example, any research he/she has done	**i.** ☐ So in today's session – I'm going to talk about the local environment, the role of local government, and also look at the interaction with the community.

You are going to listen to the introductions to three different lectures. Before you listen to each introduction, you will do some activities to help you anticipate the content of the lectures.

3.1   **The first lecture is entitled *Britain and the European Monetary Union*. Before you listen, discuss the following questions with a partner.**

1. What is the Eurozone?
2. What countries are in the Eurozone?
3. What do you think Britain's attitude to the EU is? And to the USA?

Check you understand the following phrases from the lecture.

currency	opt out	the Commonwealth

3.2   ▶ **CD1: 7 Listen to the introduction to the lecture *Britain and the European Monetary Union*. Which functions from the checklist in Task 2 does the lecturer use?**

3.3   **The second lecture is entitled *Globalization*. Before you listen, discuss the following questions with a partner.**

1. What does *globalization* mean to you?
2. What kind of people does it affect?
3. Which department of the university do you think the lecturer will be from?

Check you understand the following words and phrases from the lecture.

stockbrokers	global tycoons	sociologist	implications

3.4   ▶ **CD1: 8 Listen to the introduction to the lecture *Globalization*. Which functions from the checklist in Task 2 does the lecturer use?**

3.5   **The third lecture is entitled *Magistrates' courts*. Before you listen, discuss the following questions with a partner.**

1. How many different types of court do you have in your country?
2. What problems do the different courts deal with?

Check you understand the following phrases from the lecture.

non-criminal matters	maintenance of children	criminal offences

3.6   ▶ **CD1: 9 Listen to the introduction to the lecture *Magistrates' courts*. Which functions from the checklist in Task 2 does the lecturer use?**

Note: At the beginning of the lecture, the speaker refers to 'John', the person who has introduced her.

> **Sound advice:**
>
> Listen carefully to the introductions to all your lectures. Doing so may help you to understand the lectures better and take better notes.

Task 4	Microskills: Word stress

4.1   ▶ **CD1: 10 Listen and complete the sentence from the introduction to *Britain and the European Monetary Union*.**

> However, _____,
> I am going to spend most of the time today talking about why Britain _____
> _____, and what that said, and still says, about
> Britain's attitude in general to membership of the European Union.

Answer the following questions.
1.   Were the missing words ones you already knew?
2.   If you already knew the words, did you recognize them when you heard them? If you didn't, why didn't you recognize them?

> **Sound advice:**
> A better understanding of the reality behind the pronunciation of English will help you develop your listening skills. One aspect of pronunciation that may cause difficulties in listening is word stress and its influence on the pronunciation of vowel sounds. For example, you may not have recognized *adopt* in Ex 4.1, either because you expected a different pronunciation or because you did not hear the initial /ə/.

4.2 ▶ **CD1: 11 Listen and complete the following sentences from the introduction to** *Magistrates' courts*. **Write one word in each space.**

> So, for example, in the case of family break-up, it would involve making parental contact orders where the parents can't agree on how much _____ time each parent should have with the child.
>
> What we are mainly _____ with today is the criminal court, and that is what I am going to spend most of my time talking about this morning.

Answer the following questions.
1. How do you pronounce the words you have written?
2. The first syllable of each word is spelt the same, but in the second extract it is pronounced differently from how you might expect. Why?

4.3 **Put the words in the box into the correct column according to their** <u>stress pattern</u>.

access	account	process (n)	produce (v)	contact	context
product	protect	adapt	promise	assist	provide
connect	consume	control	consist	assume	aspect

Oo	oO
access	account

a. Now label the words in the two columns *n* (noun) or *v* (verb), where they are not labelled already.
b. Look at where the stress falls in the two-syllable words. Can you see a connection between word form and word stress in two-syllable words?

4.4   ▶ **CD1: 12 Listen to a recording about security and computers. Complete the text with one word in each space. Use forms of the words from Ex 4.3.**

Security is an important _____ of using a computer that many people do not pay much attention to. If you buy a laptop or personal computer, you will probably want to _____ to the Internet. If so, it is important that you install security software which will protect it from attack by viruses or spyware. Now there is a wide range of _____ available on the market which are relatively cheap and which _____ a variety of different features. For example, in addition to checking their computer for viruses, parents can use the software to _____ which websites their children can _____. You should not _____, however, that you are 100% safe if you are using such security software. You should make sure that you have backup copies of your work, and you should be very careful about keeping important information, such as bank _____ details, on your computer.

4.5   ▶ **CD1: 13 Listen to a recording about competition between large supermarket chains and small local shops. Complete the text with one word in each space. All the words begin with con~, pro~ or a~.**

Because of planning restrictions, the large UK supermarket chains are looking to expand their businesses and increase _____ by opening smaller 'convenience stores'. Organizations representing small, independent shops _____ that they now face unfair competition from the large chains. And they _____ the large chains of a number of practices that make it difficult for them to compete. Firstly, it is _____ that below-cost pricing is used by large supermarkets to force smaller, local shops out of business. Secondly, the large chains often buy up land which is not immediately used, and this prevents smaller local businesses from entering the market.

There is also some _____ that the large chains are treating their suppliers unfairly. Farmers claim that they are being paid less for their products, and they are reluctant to complain for fear of losing key _____.
However, supermarkets argue that the _____ is the best regulator of the market.

Look at the words you have written in the spaces. Does the stress fall on the first or second syllable? How do you pronounce these words?

4.6   **Put the words in the box into the correct column according to their stress pattern.**

decent	decide	reflect	expert	extinct	rescue
equal	reptile	defend	dentist	delay	even
effect	decline	rely	reckon	report	emerge

Oo	oO
decent	decide

4.7   ▶ **CD1: 14 Listen to a recording about the effect of global warming on numbers of polar bears. Complete the text with one word in each space. Use forms of the words from Ex 4.6.**

Wildlife _____ predict that numbers of polar bears will _____ by at least 50% over the next 50 years because of global warming. Polar bears _____ on sea ice to catch seals for food, and it has _____ that ice floes in the Arctic are disappearing at an alarming rate. Now scientists _____ that the animals are already beginning to suffer the _____ of climate change in some parts of Canada, and if there is any further _____ in tackling this problem, polar bears may be _____ by the end of the century.

4.8   ▶ **CD1: 15 Listen to a recording about monitoring water levels in rivers. Complete the text with one word in each space. All the words begin with *de~*, *re~* or *e~*.**

Scientists are now able to monitor river levels using information from satellites by using a computer programme _____ by researchers at De Montfort University in Leicester. Satellites have been able to measure the height of the sea by timing how long it takes to _____ a beam bounced back off waves. But, until now, interference from objects on the banks of rivers has made it impossible to measure river levels.

However, the new programme, which is based on data collected over the last _____, is specially _____ to filter out this interference. This new technology will be particularly useful in monitoring river levels in _____ areas. It will, for example, enable scientists to _____ river-level patterns over the _____ Amazon River basin, contributing towards our understanding of climate change.

Look at the words you have written in the spaces. Does the stress fall on the first or second syllable? How do you pronounce these words?

Unit summary

In this unit you have seen how a lecture introduction can help you to better understand the lecture and practised taking notes on introductions to lectures. You have also focused on words that may be pronounced differently from the way you expect them to be.

1 **Look at these extracts from lecture introductions. Underline the topic of each lecture.**

a. Now, you may think that a lecture entitled *Britain and the European Monetary Union* will be about Britain's plans to join the EMU, but what we will actually look at today is why Britain is not part of the Monetary Union.

b. What I especially want to focus on today is low-paid employment within the public sector, and not get sidetracked into talking about the many underpaid individuals in the private sector, or indeed, the unemployed.

c. Rather than talk at length about crime figures as a whole, I'm going to concentrate on crime that is considered to be drug-related. That means crime that occurs because the perpetrator needs to buy drugs to satisfy an addiction – crimes like burglary and common theft, for example.

2 **Complete each of these functions of lecture introductions with a word from the box below.**

approaches	content	research	scope
theory	background	interest	previous

a. limit the _____ of the lecture

b. comment on a _____

c. preview the _____ or structure of the current lecture

d. refer to _____ that has been done into the subject

e. give _____ information to the lecture topic

f. introduce different _____ to the subject

g. indicate that they are referring back to _____ lectures

h. explain the lecturer's own _____ in the subject

For web resources relevant to this book, see:
www.englishforacademicstudy.com

These weblinks will provide you with further practice in the language of introductions and help you with issues concerning word stress.

3   Identifying key ideas in lectures

In this unit you will:

- practise identifying the key points a lecturer wants to make
- distinguish key points from examples
- use your understanding of examples to deduce key points
- develop your understanding of relationships between ideas
- learn patterns of pronunciation and word stress in word families

---

Task 1   Thinking about key ideas

1.1   **Discuss the following questions with another student or in groups.**

     1. Why is it important to recognize key ideas (or main points) in a lecture?

     2. Why do lecturers use examples?

Task 2   Identifying key points in a lecture

2.1   **You are going to listen to the first part of a lecture on franchising. Before you listen, discuss the following questions with another student.**

     1. What is *franchising*?

     2. Can you think of any businesses that are run as franchises?

2.2   ▶ **CD1: 16** **Listen to Part 1 of the lecture, which is in three sections. Identify the three sections and number them in the correct order.**

☐ a definition of franchising

☐ examples of successful franchises

☐ one reason for setting up a franchise business

☐ how franchising works

☐ the types of business that are suitable for franchising

2.3 ▶ **CD1: 17 Listen to Part 1, Section 1 again and answer the questions. Check that you understand the following words and phrases before listening.**

enterprise	entrepreneur	exert control	unwilling

1. What may you need in order to develop a small or medium-sized enterprise?
2. What example of such a business is given?
3. What risks are there for a business owner in expanding his or her business?
4. Which of these is the key point made in this section? Why?
   - Expanding your business can be very risky.
   - Franchising your business can minimize the risks involved in its expansion.
   - Franchising your business can be very profitable.

2.4 ▶ **CD1: 18 Listen to Part 1, Section 2 again and answer the following questions.**

1. What type of franchising is defined here?
2. If Bill Jones wants to open a branch of McDonald's in his hometown,
   - who is the franchisor?
   - who is the franchisee?
3. What does the licence entitle the franchisee to do?
4. What would the 'package' received by the franchisee include?

2.5 ▶ **CD1: 19 Listen to Part 1, Section 3 again and answer the following questions.**

1. What does the franchisor provide to the franchisee?
2. What two kinds of fee does the franchisee pay?
3. What is the difference between these two fees?
4. Which of these is the key point made in this section?
   - That fast-food restaurants can be successful franchise businesses.
   - How the fees are calculated.
   - How each party in the business agreement benefits.

Task 3	Distinguishing key points from examples

The lecturer begins Part 2 of the lecture by saying: 'There are a number of issues that you need to consider when deciding whether or not to franchise your business.' He is looking at this from the viewpoint of the owner of a growing business trying to decide whether or not to become a franchisor.

3.1 Discuss what you think he will talk about next with another student.

3.2 ▶ **CD1: 20 Listen to Part 2 of the lecture.**

a. Make brief notes in your notebook on the key points made by the lecturer. You need to write down 5–10 words for each point.
b. Compare your notes with your partner. Have you identified the same main points?

Lecturers often use specific words or phrases (e.g., *Firstly*, *Secondly*, *Another point to remember is …*) to introduce a key point. For example, the lecturer **signposts** the first point in Part 2 by saying: '*Firstly*, there needs to be …'

3.3   **Look at the transcript for Track 20 on page 79 and find two or three examples of language used by the lecturer to signpost key points.**

3.4   ▶ **CD1: 21 Listen to Part 2, Section 1 again and answer the following questions.**
   1.   The lecturer makes the point that a relatively stable, long-term market is needed for a successful franchise operation. To support this point, the lecturer gives two reasons and two examples. What are they?
   2.   Do the examples help make his point clearer? If so, how?

3.5   ▶ **CD1: 22 Listen to Part 2, Section 2 again and answer the following questions.**
   1.   What point does he make about buying supplies in bulk?
   2.   How is this point related to the main point in this section?
   3.   Now look at the following excerpt. Having made the key point (highlighted), the speaker repeats the idea twice. Underline the words in the excerpt where he repeats the idea.

> In addition – and this is fairly obvious – ==you will need a fairly wide margin between cost and income==. Remember that the gross margin needs to provide a return on the investment to both the franchisor and the franchisee. So you will need to keep costs low and prices as high as the market will bear. One advantage of a franchise operation is that supplies can be bought in bulk across the whole franchise, which will help to keep costs down. But you can see that franchising would be unsuitable in a market where the margin between cost and income is very narrow.

3.6   ▶ **CD1: 23 Listen to Part 2, Section 3 again and answer the following questions.**
   1.   What does the franchisor need to provide to the franchisee?
   2.   When are these required?
   3.   What point is made about franchisees in the restaurant industry?
   4.   What do you think is the key point in this section?

Task 4	Signposting and highlighting key points

In Part 3, the lecturer continues to discuss some of the issues that need to be considered when deciding whether or not to franchise your business.

4.1   ▶ **CD1: 24 Listen to Part 3 of the lecture. Make notes on the key points in your notebook. Then compare your notes with another student. Have you identified the same key points?**

4.2 ▶ **CD1: 25** Listen to Part 3, Section 1 again and complete the excerpt with one to three words in each space.

> One further issue you may need to consider is whether the business is _____
> to another geographical area. If you have developed your business serving one
> particular part of the country and you want to set up a franchise network covering a
> _____ – the whole country, for example – another thing you
> will have to consider is whether there is a _____ for your
> product or service in different regions. It may be, for example, that competition in
> other parts of the country may be so _____ that it is difficult for
> franchisees to _____, or that for localized _____ or
> _____ reasons the business may not be as profitable.

4.3 ▶ **CD1: 26** Listen to Part 3, Section 2 again.
   a.   Underline the signposting language used to highlight key points.
   b.   Now listen again and circle any key words or phrases the lecturer stresses.

> Finally, when you are setting up a franchise
> network, you will need to bear in mind that you will
> be losing direct control of the way your brand is
> perceived by the customer, so this brings me to my
> last point, which is to emphasize the importance of
> protecting your brand. I am sure you are all aware
> that it often takes a long time to establish a
> distinctive brand with a valuable reputation, but
> that this reputation can be damaged comparatively
> quickly if, for example, quality standards are not
> consistently applied. The detailed operating manual
> that I referred to earlier will play a role in maintaining the brand but, just as important,
> you need to take care selecting franchisees and monitoring their operations. In addition
> to checking that franchisees have the relevant skills and experience to run a successful
> business, you also need to ensure that they share the same business values as you, that
> they accept the importance of maintaining the brand and that they are clear about
> what they can or can't change about the way the business is run – so people who are
> very individualistic will probably not make good franchisees.

Study tip

Lecturers often use signposting
language to indicate the start of
a new point.

Techniques to highlight ideas
include:

* stressing key words or
  phrases
* pausing after key words or
  phrases

4.4 ▶ **CD1: 27 Listen to Part 3, Section 3 again and complete the notes in as much detail as you think is necessary.**

<u>Protecting the brand</u>

Written agreement should specify

Initial training – to ensure staff

Regular visits – to ensure

Ongoing training – to deal with

Protecting the brand is in the interests of

Which of the techniques that the lecturer used helped you to complete the notes?

Sound advice:
- As you listen, try to keep in mind the key ideas and relate any new information you hear to those ideas.
- Listen for signposting language, stressed words or phrases and pauses as indicators of key points.
- If you do not understand a key point, listen for any examples which may help you to recover the meaning.
- Remember that effective lecturers sometimes repeat key points. This gives you time to note them down, but try to avoid writing down the same idea twice!

You can extend your vocabulary by learning groups of words which have the same basic form and which are often related in meaning.

5.1 **Practise the pronunciation of the words in the table and underline the stressed syllable in each word.**

Examples:

Noun	Verb	Adjective
product, production, productivity	produce	productive
definition	define	definite, definitive
economy, economics, economist	economize	economic, economical

5.2 **Use the words in the table to study how changes in syllable stress within word families affect pronunciation.**

In many cases, a different syllable stress has an effect on the pronunciation of the sounds.

Example:

product   /ˈprɒdʌkt/

produce   /prəˈdjuːs/

5.3 ▶ **CD1: 28 You can also modify the meaning of a word by adding a prefix, e.g., *interpret/misinterpret*, *assess/reassess*, *appear/disappear*. Listen to the sentences and write in the missing prefix to each word.**

How do the prefixes change the meaning of the original words?

> **Study tip**
>
> If you think about the grammar *and* meaning of each sentence as you do the exercise, you are more likely to get the correct answers.

1. All trade unions were declared _____ legal by the government.

2. This is one example of a _____ match between the individual's goals and those of the organization.

3. They found no significant _____ relation between class size and levels of achievement.

4. Real estate _____ actions rose by 30% last month.

5. Prices are determined through the _____ action of supply and demand.

6. These animals exhibited _____ normal behaviour compared with the control group.

5.4 ▶ **CD1: 29 Listen to the sentences and complete them with two to four words in each space. Some of the words include prefixes.**

1. We had to get the _____ because the detail was not very clear on the original ones.

2. Many doctors work _____, which put them under a lot of stress.

3. Crime prevention is _____ of the police's work, but it is often difficult to assess its effectiveness.

4. Doctors have noticed an _____, such as bulimia and anorexia, not just among young women but, surprisingly, among young men.

5. These plants should be grown in partial shade, rather than _____.

6. Researchers have found that _____ much more likely to be involved in traffic accidents.

5.5 ▶ **CD1: 30 Listen to the groups of sentences. Complete the sentences with two to four words in each space. One of the words in each space is a form of the word in bold.**

1. a. Children need a **secure** environment in which to grow up.

   b. Many immigrants are only able to find _____.

   c. The money was invested in _____ and property.

2. a. Achievement levels **vary** considerably from school to school in the city.

   b. Some economists believe that interest rates can be predicted by examining _____.

   c. In the Eden Project they have managed to create _____ habitats.

   d. There is _____ to health care in different parts of the country.

3. a. How are we going to **solve** this problem?

   b. You need to _____ in water before applying it to the crop.

   c. There appears to be _____ between the two countries, despite years of peace negotiations.

4. a. A mass spectrometer was used to **analyze** the gases.

    b. _____ of the data is needed to confirm these initial findings.

    c. The course is designed to help students to develop _____ _____.

5. a. The results **indicate** that the virus mutates more rapidly than was first believed.

    b. All the _____ suggest that the economy is recovering.

    c. The strike was _____ the level of the workers' frustration.

6. a. Chomsky was a fierce **critic** of Bush Senior's foreign policy.

    b. There was _____ _____ the way the election had been administered.

    c. The negotiations _____ _____ establishment of peace in the area.

Sound advice:

Your listening skills will improve if you work to enlarge your vocabulary. Learning word families is an effective way of doing this, but you also need to develop your awareness of differences in pronunciation between words in each family. You can learn the most useful word families by referring to the **Academic Word List** and by doing the exercises in *EAS: Vocabulary*.

Unit summary

In this unit you have practised identifying key points in a lecture and have seen how examples can help you understand a key point. You have also developed your understanding of relationships between ideas and learnt patterns of pronunciation and word stress in word families.

1   **Which two statements about how a lecturer identifies key points in a lecture are not true? Tick (✓) these two false statements.**

   a.   The lecturer may use signposting words and phrases to indicate a key point. ☐

   b.   The lecturer may use words and phrases that are specific to the topic of the lecture. ☐

   c.   The lecturer may stress important words and phrases. ☐

   d.   The lecturer may pause for a moment before introducing a key point. ☐

   e.   The lecturer may repeat some key points. ☐

   f.   The lecturer may speak very quickly at times to emphasize that a point is key. ☐

   g.   The lecturer may give examples to support a key point. ☐

   h.   The lecturer may give reasons why a point is important. ☐

2   **Tick the statement below that is true for you.**

   a.   I can now distinguish between key points and examples. ☐

   b.   I still get confused about the difference between key points and examples. ☐

3   **When a lecturer uses typical words and phrases to indicate a key point, it is called signposting. Write eight signposting words and phrases from the unit here.**

   _____   _____

   _____   _____

   _____   _____

   _____   _____

For web resources relevant to this book, see:
www.englishforacademicstudy.com

These weblinks will help you identify and practise key vocabulary and provide you with further listening practice related to business matters and franchising.

4 Note-taking: Part 1

In this unit you will:
- discuss the reasons for taking notes in a lecture
- learn the principles of effective note-taking
- practise taking notes from lectures

Task 1   Reasons for taking notes

1.1   **Discuss the following questions with another student.**
1. Why do students take notes in lectures?
2. What do they do with the notes after lectures?
3. Why will the volume and focus of the notes vary from one student to another?
4. When you are taking notes, what kind of information do you need to write down? What do you not need to write down?

Task 2   Principles of note-taking

2.1   **You are going to listen to an extract from a lecture on dealing with traffic problems in the UK. Before you listen, discuss the following questions.**
1. Why do you think there are so many cars on the roads in Britain?
2. What kind of problems does this create?
3. Can you think of any ways of reducing the amount of traffic on Britain's roads? What are they?

2.2   ▶ **CD1: 31 Listen to the recording and read the extract from the transcript at the same time.**

Part 1

So Britain's roads, and especially those in the south-east, are overcrowded. There are too many cars on the roads, and at particular times of the day and particular places, traffic is either very slow or at a standstill. Now, this has a number of effects. Firstly, there is the economic effect, all the time wasted in traffic jams, which means a loss of productivity. Then there's the environmental effect. Cars produce a lot of pollution, which damages the local environment, but it also contributes to global warming. And there's also an effect on people's health. In addition to the poor air quality and the damage this causes people's lungs, the stress of being stuck in traffic each day leads to higher risk of heart disease.

2.3 **Look at the following notes taken by a student during the lecture. Then answer the questions below.**

> UK's roads overcrowded ➡ effects
>
>   – economic; loss of prod.vity
>   – environmental; pollution, glob. warming
>   – health probs.; lung, heart disease

1. Why has the student chosen this information to note down?
2. From your reading of the lecture extract, is there anything else the student should have noted down?
3. Are the notes clear? When the student reads the notes a week later, will she be able to understand them?
4. What techniques did the student use to:
   a. make sure the notes are clear?
   b. save time?

2.4 **Look at how the student has selected the key ideas from what the lecturer said. The extract has been annotated to show what she omitted from her notes.**

Unimportant information

> So Britain's roads, ~~and especially those in the south-east,~~ are overcrowded. ~~There are too many cars on the roads, and at particular times of the day and particular places, traffic is either very slow or at a standstill.~~ Now, this has a number of effects.

Repetition of ideas expressed
in previous sentence

Notes: UK's roads overcrowded → effects

2.5 ▶ **CD1: 32–CD1: 35 What do you think the speaker will discuss in the rest of the lecture?**

Listen to Parts 2–5 of the lecture and make notes on page 34. Before you listen to each part of the lecture, check you understand the meaning and pronunciation of the words in the boxes.

Part 2

policy	measure (n)	politically sensitive

_____

_____

_____

Part 3

integrated	investment

_____

_____

_____

Part 4

(road) lane	CCTV	congestion

_____

_____

_____

Part 5

pressure	scheme	coalition

_____

_____

_____

> **Sound advice:**
>
> When taking notes, you need to be:
> - **selective:** decide what is important according to the speaker and according to your knowledge of the subject.
> - **brief:** use **abbreviations** and symbols.
> - **clear:** make sure the relationships between ideas are clearly related to each other.
>
> When you read the notes some time later, will you understand them?

Task 3   Note-taking practice

You are going to listen to extracts from a lecture on the history of development economics and practise taking notes.

3.1   **Before you listen, discuss the following questions with another student.**

   1. Which East Asian countries have developed rapidly since the 1990s?
   2. Can you explain the reasons for this rapid economic growth?

   Check you understand the meaning and pronunciation of the words and phrases in the boxes before you listen to each section.

3.2   ▶ **CD1: 36 In Part 1 of the extract, the lecturer is discussing the reasons for rapid economic growth in East Asia in the 1990s. Listen and continue the following notes.**

   Note: Remember to be *selective*, *brief* and *clear*.

   Part 1

liberalism	intervention

   Interpreting East Asian economic miracle.

   Dispute about influence of market liberalism,

   e.g., China ...

3.3 ▶ **CD1: 37** In Part 2 of the extract, the lecturer goes on to discuss another factor. Listen to Part 2 and continue the notes.

Part 2

labour rates	stimulus

Everyone agreed about one element –

_____

_____

_____

Task 4	**Microskills: Sentence stress**

In Unit 3 you saw how word stress affects the pronunciation of syllables in the word. In a similar way, in any spoken **utterance**, certain words are stressed, and this affects the pronunciation of other words in the utterance.

4.1 ▶ **CD1: 38** Listen to this extract from Track 37. The main stressed words in this sentence are marked in bold.

> …, that you could **always** hire a lot of people at **low** labour rates, but who were in reasonably good **health**, who were **literate** and who had reasonable **skills**.

Note: The speaker chooses to stress words which are particularly important to what he is saying. These tend to be **content words**, rather than **function words**.

One problem in listening is that often the *unstressed words* tend to be:
- pronounced in unexpected ways, e.g., *that* /ðət/ and *were* /wə/
- compressed together in fast speech, so that it is difficult to hear where one word ends and another begins, e.g., *a lot of people* /əlɒtəvpiːpəl/

4.2 ▶ **CD1: 39** Listen to the following sentence from Track 36.

> The **Japanese** _____ **never** run _____ purely free-market economy. **Neither** _____ the **Koreans**.

a. Complete the sentences with one word in each space.
b. The missing words are function words which are unstressed.
   - How easy or difficult was it to hear these words?
   - If it was difficult, could you work out what they were from the context?

4.3   ▶ **CD1: 40 Read the following extract from a lecture about market research. Listen to the extract and complete the sentences with two to seven words in each space.**

Note: The lecturer is making the point that when you are collecting market research data through a questionnaire, you need to test out the questionnaire on a small number of people to check that it works well before you carry out the real survey.

You need to pre-test the questionnaire. This is really important. Those of you, some of you, will be doing this for, you know, your dissertation. Some of you, I know,
_____. You need to pre-test the thing, because you're the researcher. You're very _____. You know what you're talking about, but you've got to check that other people do as well. And if you want a statistically valid sample of a hundred or two hundred people,
_____ you're collecting the data properly. And it's here that these _____, they're going to tell you whether it's going to work or not.

So make sure that you do pilots and, you know, this can be, sort of, _____
_____ different people that you question. I mean, you'll soon find out whether you've got any potential … or any doubts about the length of the questionnaire, _____,
or whether the sort of questions that you're asking are valid. You'll soon find out from that. So, piloting or pre-testing is really important.

4.4   **Look at the words that you wrote in the spaces in Ex 4.3 and answer the following questions.**
1.   Which words were stressed?
2.   What kind of words were unstressed? How were these words pronounced? Was it difficult to hear them?

Sound advice:
Some of the missing words in Ex 4.3 are unstressed and difficult to hear. Because they are function words, you do not always need to understand them to follow the meaning. However, function words often show the relationships between ideas in the sentence, so there can be times when it is important to understand them correctly.

Unit summary

In this unit you have discussed why it is important to take notes during a lecture and worked on your note-taking skills. You have also become more familiar with sentence stress and the difficulties of hearing unstressed words.

1 **Underline the correct option in each of these pieces of advice about effective note-taking.**

   a. During a lecture, you need to *write down everything you hear / be selective about what you write down.*

   b. You should try to *keep notes brief / write a lot to please your lecturer.*

   c. You need to make sure that *you / your lecturer* can understand the notes at a later date.

   d. You *must write down key words related to the topic / don't need to write down key words because you will remember them anyway.*

   e. You should *always use full sentences and complete words / sometimes use abbreviations to save time.*

   f. You should *make sure that the way points relate to one another is clear / note down points randomly because it is the quickest way to do it.*

2 **Complete each of these statements so that they are true for you. Delete any words you don't need.**

   a. I am happy that the notes I take usually _____.

   b. When I look back at my notes later, I _____.

   c. My notes are sometimes too _____.

   d. I would like my notes to be (more) _____.

3 **Look at this sentence and then answer the questions that follow.**

> It is important for you to learn how to take notes effectively during a lecture.

   a. Can you identify the three main stressed syllables in the sentence above?

   b. How quickly can you identify words that are weakened and more difficult to hear?

   c. Why is it useful to be aware of stressed words and syllables when you are listening to lectures?

For web resources relevant to this book, see:
www.englishforacademicstudy.com

These weblinks will provide you with further help in note-taking, as well as information in lecture format on a number of topics, including sentence stress.

5 Note-taking: Part 2

In this unit you will:

- learn how to use abbreviations and symbols to save time when note-taking
- discuss the advantages and disadvantages of two ways of taking notes
- practise note-taking from lectures

Task 1 — Returning to your notes

It is important to make clear notes during lectures, as you will need to understand them after the lecture or when you refer back to them later in the year. It is useful to look at the way others make notes, but in the end you will develop your own style.

Your teacher will show you some notes from a lecture extract that you listened to in Unit 4.

1.1 **See how you can expand the notes into complete sentences with another student.**

As you discuss, try to explain how the ideas are connected to one another.

> **Study tip**
>
> Remember that you will need your notes for future reference, so make sure they are clearly understandable.

Task 2 — Using abbreviations and symbols

2.1 **What abbreviations and symbols were used in the notes in Task 1, and what do they mean?**

2.2 **Look at the examples of abbreviations that an economics student used. What do you think they stand for?**

> **Study tip**
>
> Your notes are generally for yourself, so the abbreviations you use will tend to be personal.

infl. _____   invest. _____   recess. _____

bus. _____   org. _____   min. _____

What abbreviations would you use if you were listening to lectures in your own field? List them below.

_____   _____

_____   _____

_____   _____

2.3 What do you think the following symbols refer to?

Symbol	Meaning	Symbol	Meaning
↗	increase, rise, go up	≠	
↘		€	
→		?	
←		!	
≥			

Task 3 — Note-taking practice

You are going to listen to extracts from two different lectures and practise note-taking using symbols and abbreviations.

3.1 ▶ **CD1: 41 Listen to a lecturer talking about language learning. She refers to a source text (Littlewood, 1992) which provides an analysis of the purposes of education in general. Continue the following notes.**

Extract 1

3 purposes of education (Littlewood, 1992)

_____

_____

_____

_____

_____

_____

3.2   ▶ **CD1: 42** **You are going to hear another extract from the lecture on development economics. Here the lecturer is describing changes in the world economy during the 1970s. Listen and continue the following notes.**

Check you understand the meaning and pronunciation of the words in the boxes before you listen.

Extract 2

boom	inflation	devalue	float

early 70s econ. boom ➔ infl. in world econ.

Task 4	**Organizing your notes**

Different people organize their notes in different ways. Some students write **linear notes**, starting at the top of the page and working down, while other students prefer to use **mind maps**. The best solution may be to use different ways of taking notes for different types of lectures.

4.1   **Look at the following descriptions of different lectures. Do you think it would be better to use mind maps or linear notes for these lectures? Why? Discuss your ideas with another student.**

1. This is a lecture on global warming. The lecturer discusses the evidence that global warming is taking place, then looks at the causes, and finally looks at possible solutions and the difficulties of solving the problem.

2. This is a lecture on teleworking. The lecturer compares teleworking with normal ways of working, i.e., office-based working. He looks at the social, financial and environmental effects/benefits of both types of work.

3. This is a lecture on the history of the European Union from the 1950s to the present day.

4. This is the first lecture in a series entitled *Global problems*. In this lecture, the speaker gives an overview of some of the main problems facing the world today.

4.2 ▶ **CD1: 43 Listen to this extract from a lecture entitled *Health in the UK* and make notes. Work with your partner. One of you should take notes in a linear style, the other should make a mind map.**

a. Before you listen, make sure you understand the words and phrases in the box. How would you abbreviate them?

individuals	life expectancy	statistics
_____	_____	_____
heart disease	prescriptions	blood pressure
_____	_____	_____
cholesterol	physical inactivity	British Heart Foundation
_____	_____	_____

b. Compare your notes with your partner. Which style of note-taking do you think was more appropriate for this lecture? Why?

4.3 **Discuss the advantages and disadvantages of linear notes and mind maps with your partner. Think about the following:**
1. the process of writing notes in a lecture
2. referring to the notes after the lecture

4.4 **Compare your opinions with another pair.**

Task 5	Microskills: Word boundaries

5.1 ▶ **CD1: 44 Listen and complete the sentences.**

1. The government has introduced _____ to encourage investment in this region.

2. For _____ these organizations are often regarded as charities.

3. A number of reforms to the _____ have been proposed.

Did you find it difficult to understand the missing words in the sentences? If so, why?

> **Sound advice**
> The pronunciation of a word is affected by the word before or after it. When you are listening, it is sometimes difficult to hear when one word ends and another begins, because it may sound as if the words are linked together. In addition, sometimes sounds are inserted between the words, or sounds disappear or change. These make pronunciation easier for the speaker, but may cause problems for the listener!

5.2   ▶ **CD1: 45 Read the explanation below and listen to the examples.**

Linked words: Consonant + vowel

When a word ends in a consonant sound and the next word begins with a vowel sound, the words may seem to be linked, e.g.,:

add‿up

What‿are these?

the main‿objective

Inserted sounds: Vowel + vowel

When a word ends with a vowel sound and the next word begins with a vowel sound, a /w/, /j/ or /r/ sound may seem to be inserted, e.g.,:

do /w/ anything

try /j/ out

no /w/ idea /r/ of it

Disappearing/changing sounds: Consonant + consonant

When a word ends with a /d/ or /t/ sound and the next word begins with a consonant, the /d/ or /t/ sound often disappears, e.g.,:

next̸ day

rapid̸ growth

5.3   ▶ **CD1: 46 Listen to the phrases. Mark the phrases with the symbols (‿), (/), /d/ and /t/ from Ex 5.2.**

1. they   invested   in   property

2. a   mixture   of   oil   and   residues

3. it's   an   open   market

4. it's   due   on   Friday   morning

5. free   admission   on   Sundays

6. it   shows   as   a   white   mark

5.4 ▶ **CD1: 47 You are going to listen to an extract from a lecture on the theory of real options in investment.**

Note: *Real options* are techniques that allow investments to be analyzed, while taking flexibility and uncertainty into account.

Listen and complete the text with two to five words in each space. The missing expressions include examples of word boundaries that may cause you difficulties.

I'm going to go through the theory of real options, and then I'm going to show you how they can be used to _____, particularly on property assets. 'Real options' is a term which was coined ten or 15 years ago, when people began to realize that _____ isn't the only thing you should look at in valuing assets, that a number of assets in companies have _____ option value. And so the option theory you've been looking at can also be applied to _____ instead of just _____. And that, in raising money, companies particularly have _____ from an option pricing perspective than they first thought. The idea of real options is that management is not just a passive participant, but that management can take _____ in making and revising decisions that can lead on from unexpected market developments such as, for example, the _____ has gone up from about $85 a barrel to _____ $100 a barrel over the last year. So, if you were an oil producer this time last year, you would be taking a very different view on the _____. So the increase in oil prices has uncovered _____ which make oil producers a lot more valuable, and now you can bring oilfields _____ that were not necessarily economic. So this is the kind of idea that when we're looking at a project, we're not just looking _____, we're actually looking at a cash flow that can be subject to a lot of optionality.

Unit summary

In this unit you have seen how abbreviations and symbols can be used when taking notes, and you have discussed the advantages and disadvantages of two ways of taking notes. You have also looked at linking and word boundaries.

1 **Circle 1, 2 or 3 to complete each of these statements about note-taking.**

a. Using abbreviations and symbols …

1. saves time.
2. shows that you are intelligent.
3. stops other students using your notes.

b. If you use abbreviations and symbols, …

1. everyone must understand them.
2. your lecturer must understand them.
3. you must understand them.

2 **Delete the wrong options in this statement so that it is true for you.**

I *don't know how to use any / can use a few / use a number of* abbreviations and symbols when I take notes.

3 **Mark each of the different lecture types a–e below as follows.**

L – I think making linear notes is the better approach.

M – I think making a mind map is the better approach.

a. The lecture compares how successful one thing is compared with another and examines the reasons. ☐

b. The lecture runs through the history of an organization. ☐

c. The lecture is on an issue that affects everyone. It also gives examples of how the issue affects particular people in particular places. ☐

d. The lecture is about a successful person and outlines what he achieved in his life. ☐

e. The lecture states that a problem exists, examines its causes and then proposes some solutions. ☐

For web resources relevant to this book, see:
www.englishforacademicstudy.com

These weblinks will provide you with help on note-taking as well as a variety of ideas for making mind maps.

6 Introducing new terminology

In this unit you will:

- listen to different lecturers introducing new terms or concepts
- meet different techniques for introducing new concepts
- practise recognizing unstressed function words which may be difficult to hear

Task 1   Introducing new terminology

Lecturers usually introduce new **terminology** to their students during lectures. The terms they introduce often represent new and quite abstract concepts which can be difficult to grasp.

Here are some of the things lecturers do to help their students understand new terms or concepts.

- ■ Give definitions.
- ■ Provide a number of extended examples.
- ■ Explain how the term or concept works.
- ■ Contrast the new concept with a concept that is already familiar to the students.

In this unit you will listen to extracts from three lectures to see how lecturers deal with the issue of new terminology.

1.1   **Think about your own experience of lectures involving new terminology. How did the lecturer deal with it? What problems, if any, did you encounter? Discuss your experience with another student.**

Task 2   Embedded words

In the following extract from a lecture on linguistics, the idea of **embedded words** is introduced by the lecturer. She gives an extended example of one embedded word to help explain the idea.

2.1   ▶ **CD2: 1 Listen to the extract and make notes.**

Embedded words:

_____

_____

_____

2.2   **Check your notes with another student. How would you define embedded words?**

2.3   **Think of at least one other example of an embedded word.**

Task 3	Introducing terms and concepts (1)

In this lecture, the speaker looks at two different types of law within the European Union: directives and regulations. Before she explains the differences between the two types of law, she reminds the audience of some of the 'key players' in the EU:

- the European Commission – a kind of civil service
- the Council of Ministers – a body that consists of the national ministers from each of the member states
- the European Parliament – which has 754 members elected from all the EU countries

3.1   **Before you listen, check that you understand the following phrases.**

minor technical matters	regulations come into force	opt out
visas and political asylum	become legally binding	pass a law

To explain the terms *regulations* and *directives* and the differences between them, the speaker talks about:

- who can issue them
- what matters the two types of law deal with
- when they become legally binding

3.2   ▶ **CD2: 2 Listen to the extract and complete the table.**

	Matters they deal with	Who issues them	When they become legally binding
Regulations			
Directives			

3.3   **Work with another student. Using your notes from the table, take it in turns to explain fully what the terms *regulations* and *directives* mean.**

In this lecture, the speaker defines what he means by *dominance*. He does this partly by contrasting this new term with a term the students already know, *monopoly*.

4.1   **Discuss the meaning of the following words with a partner.**

    1.   dominance   **2.**   monopoly

4.2   **Before you listen, check that you understand the following phrases.**

in sole control	not vulnerable to competition
a sizeable market share	the second-largest firm

4.3   ▶ **CD2: 3** **Listen to the extract and make notes on the lecturer's definitions of both terms.**

Monopoly

_____

_____

_____

Dominance

_____

_____

_____

4.4   **Work with your partner. What examples of monopolies and dominant firms can you think of?**

Task 5	Microskills: Weak forms of function words

5.1 ▶ **CD2: 4** Listen to the following pairs of sentences. What is the difference in the pronunciation of the bold words in each pair? What might explain this difference?

1.　a.　What time **does** the train leave?

　　b.　I'm not sure why he's late. He **does** know about the meeting.

2.　a.　**Some** researchers have taken a different approach.

　　b.　We've just got time for **some** questions.

3.　a.　It was heated to 150°C **for** ten minutes.

　　b.　There are arguments **for** and against GM crop trials.

4.　a.　I'm not sure what you're getting **at**.

　　b.　There were **at** least five errors in the programme.

5.　a.　Increasingly, small memory devices **can** store large amounts of data.

　　b.　Well, I **can** do it, but I don't want to.

6.　a.　Oh, are they going to interview **us** as well as the students?

　　b.　Can you tell **us** what you've found?

5.2 Look back at the words in bold in Ex 5.1. Normally these words are unstressed. Why has the speaker chosen the stressed form in certain sentences?

In the following extract from the lecture about market research, the lecturer is discussing the advantages and disadvantages of using multiple-choice questions.

> **Study tip**
>
> Many function words, such as conjunctions, articles, prepositions and auxiliary verbs, are difficult to hear when they are unstressed.

5.3 ▶ **CD2: 5** Listen and complete the extract with three to five words in each space. In each case, at least one of the missing words is a function word.

> Multiple-choice questions – dead easy. They reduce interviewer bias; very easy for people to … very easy and fast for people to answer; very _____ _____. But the argument goes that they are rather difficult to design. The thing about multiple-choice questions is that _____ people into certain answers. This is a good _____. If you have a multiple-choice question and you pilot it, you may find that people are not, they don't put the issue that you're asking them into that particular _____ that you've imposed. So that's where _____ will help. Let me just show you an example of this.

Unit summary

In this unit you have listened to different lecturers introducing new terms or concepts and met different techniques for introducing new concepts. You have also practised recognizing unstressed function words which may be difficult to hear.

1 **A lecturer has introduced the term _hire purchase_. Match the techniques he/she could use to make the term clear (a–d) with the extracts (1–4).**

   a. Give a definition. ☐

   b. Provide an example. ☐

   c. Explain how something works. ☐

   d. Contrast the new concept with a concept that is already familiar to the students. ☐

   1. The person buying the product pays for it over a period of time instead of paying for it all in one go. They might make six payments of £200 or 12 payments of £100. Usually they will have to pay interest on top, and that is why retailers are keen on the system.

   2. Now, you all know what a loan is. You borrow money and pay it back at a later date. Hire purchase is a sort of loan, but …

   3. Hire purchase is one way that people can buy something – usually a fairly expensive product – in a way that they can afford. They make a number of payments instead of one large payment.

   4. Say somebody wants a new sofa, but cannot afford to pay one sum of £2,000. Well, one way round this is to …

2 **Underline the technique a–d that you have found most helpful so far when trying to understand new concepts.**

3 **Look at this sentence and then answer the questions that follow.**

> There are a number of different ways that a lecturer can make new concepts easier for students to understand.

   a. How many function words can you identify in the sentence above that would probably be unstressed in normal speech?

   b. Write five more function words in your notebook.

   c. Why is it useful to be aware of unstressed function words when you are listening to lectures?

For web resources relevant to this book, see:
www.englishforacademicstudy.com

These weblinks will provide you with further practice in listening to short talks on issues of global concern.

7   What lecturers do in lectures

In this unit you will:

- think about how lecturers organize information in their lectures
- discuss other ways of organizing information
- practise note-taking
- learn how word stress and pronunciation vary within word families

Task 1   Macrostructure of lectures

Writers use different structures to organize their writing. For example, they might use this structure.

In a similar way, lecturers may also use different structures to organize their lectures. Here are some examples of what lecturers might do during a lecture.

Lecture structure 1	**Lecture structure 2**	**Lecture structure 3**
suggest alternative methods of doing something ↓ discuss the benefits and drawbacks of each method	state a hypothesis ↓ outline an experiment to test the hypothesis ↓ look at the results of the experiment ↓ draw conclusions from the results	present a theory ↓ see how the theory works in practice ↓ suggest problems with the theory

Sound advice:

Recognizing the structure of a lecture may help you understand the main ideas that the lecturer is trying to communicate. As you listen to a lecture, ask yourself:

- What is the lecturer doing at this point in the lecture?
- How does this part of the lecture relate to the other parts of the lecture?

These questions will help you get the 'big picture' – i.e., the main ideas – of the lecturer's argument.

1.1   **Think of lectures you have listened to. Discuss the following questions in groups.**

    1.   Can you think of any lectures where the lecturers used these structures?

    2.   Can you think of any other ways in which lecturers organize their lectures?

Task 2	Lecture structure (1): Doing market research

In the lecture you are going to listen to, the speaker is outlining different methods that market researchers use to get information from people. She also discusses the implications of each method.

2.1 **Before you listen, discuss the following questions in groups.**

1. Have you ever been asked to take part in a market research survey? What did you have to do? What kind of market research was it?
2. What do you think are the main ways of carrying out market research?
3. What are some advantages and disadvantages of each of the methods?

2.2 ▶ **CD2: 6 The lecturer talks about four methods of market research in this lecture. Listen and complete the list of methods that she mentions.**

- computer-assisted telephone interviewing (CATI)

- _____

- _____

- _____

2.3 ▶ **CD2: 6 Listen again and make notes in your notebook on any implications she mentions for any of the methods.**

Task 3	Lecture structure (2): Social learning

In the lecture you are going to listen to next, the speaker is looking at the hypothesis suggesting that animals learn from each other, for example, learning which foods to eat or avoid and which animals are their natural predators.

The lecturer discusses various experiments which have been used to test this hypothesis. She describes an experiment where a researcher took a group of 'naïve' monkeys that had been brought up in zoos. The monkeys had never encountered snakes and thus had no fear of them. These naïve monkeys first observed a group of wild monkeys who were afraid of snakes. The researcher then tested the monkeys to see if their behaviour had changed.

3.1 **Before you listen, discuss the following questions in groups.**

1. Do you think animals learn from each other? What do they learn and how?
2. What kind of experiments do you think researchers do to test social learning?

3.2   ▶ **CD2: 7 Listen to Part 1 of the extract describing how the experiments were carried out. Complete the notes.**

<u>Hypothesis:</u>

Monkeys in the wild learn to fear snakes from other monkeys who've already

acquired the fear.

<u>Experimental situation:</u>

Observer monkeys

<u>Timetable of experiment:</u>

Pre-test

Post-test

Follow-up test

3.3 Label the two diagrams with these phrases: *neutral stimulus, glass box, food, model snake*. You will need to use some of the phrases more than once.

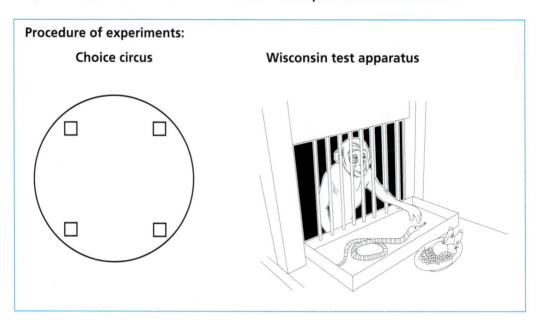

Procedure of experiments:

Choice circus   Wisconsin test apparatus

3.4 ▶ **CD2: 8 Listen to Part 2 of the extract. Make notes on the results and the conclusion the speaker draws from the results.**

Note: When giving the results, the speaker refers to a graph.

Results:

The demonstrators (the monkeys brought up in the wild):

_____

_____

The observers (the monkeys brought up in zoos):

_____

_____

_____

Conclusion:

_____

_____

_____

_____

| Task 4 | Lecture structure (3): Contestable markets |

In the next lecture, the speaker is talking about *contestable markets*. He defines them as markets where entry and exit barriers do not exist or are low; in other words, it is easy or cheap for new suppliers to come into the market, and so existing suppliers have to worry about potential competition. The airline industry is commonly given as an example of such a market – especially now that there are many low-cost airlines.

The speaker begins by talking about the *theory* of perfect contestability and what the theory predicts. He then discusses the *problem* with this theory.

4.1 **Before you listen, check that you understand the meaning of the following words and phrases.**

marginal costs	incur sunk costs	monopoly price	oligopolies
in excess of	inevitable delays	undercut the price	

Do you think contestable markets are good for:
1. the consumers?
2. firms already in the market?
3. firms that would like to come into the market?

4.2 ▶ **CD2: 9 Listen to the extract and complete the notes.**

Note: The speaker uses the term *incumbent firm* to refer to companies that are already in the market and the terms *an entry* and *the entrant* to refer to companies that would like to come into the market.

What the theory predicts:
_____
_____
_____
_____

Problems with the theory:
_____
_____
_____
_____

Task 5	Microskills: Word families (2)

Many nouns can be formed from verbs by adding a suffix. There may also be small changes in the spelling and pronunciation.

Example:

Verb	Noun
describe /dɪsˈkraɪb/	description /dɪsˈkrɪpʃn/
prefer /prɪˈfɜː/	preference /ˈprefrəns/
propose /prəˈpəʊz/	proposal /prəˈpəʊzl/

5.1 **Change the verbs in the box into nouns and write them in the appropriate column in the table.**

conclude	require	remove	fail	integrate	exist
dismiss	deduce	consume	acquire	proceed	amend
achieve	approve	compete	convert	resist	combine

~tion/~sion	~ance/~ence	~ment	~al	~ure

5.2 You will sometimes find that speakers use both verb and noun forms from the same **word family** in close proximity to one another. Here is an example.

Although we had **decided** to focus our research on a limited range of fungi, it was a **decision** we were later forced to reassess.

▶ **CD2: 10 Listen to the following short lecture extracts.**
a.   Make notes on the main points in the table below.
b.   Listen again for a verb and noun from the same family in each extract.

Topic	Your notes	Verb and noun from same family
1. earthquakes in the UK		
2. hospital workers and radiation		
3. Japan's electronics industry		
4. poverty		
5. behaviour of particles		
6. road safety schemes		
7. male lions in Africa		
8. financial products		

5.3 ▶ **CD2: 11 You may find that, rather than using a verb and noun from the same family, in some cases, you will hear synonyms. Listen to the following short texts and complete them with words or phrases that are synonyms.**

1. Many people are _____ that young people lack strong role models, and this _____ has prompted the police to question the conduct of professional footballers, whose actions may have a significant influence on young men.

2. The USA decided to _____ the Moscow Olympics in 1980, in protest at the Soviet Union's invasion of Afghanistan. Four years later, the Soviet Union retaliated with its own _____ of the Los Angeles Olympics.

3. Many multinational companies prefer to _____ local enterprises. Such _____ have a number of advantages.

4. The public's _____ of the government's handling of the economy was critical. While the economy had in fact grown by 2%, people _____ the high unemployment rate and the government's inability to control strikes as indicators of poor performance.

Unit summary

In this unit you have looked at different ways that information in a lecture can be organized and practised listening to lectures organized in different ways. You have also learnt about word stress within word families.

1 **Think of three ways that the logical organization of a lecture helps you to understand and take notes.**

a. _____

b. _____

c. _____

2 **Put the stages of these two lectures into a logical order.**

Lecture 1
a. look at the results of the experiment
b. draw conclusions from the results
c. state a hypothesis
d. outline an experiment to test the hypothesis

1 ☐   2 ☐   3 ☐   4 ☐

Lecture 2
a. see how the theory works in practice
b. suggest problems with the theory
c. present a theory

1 ☐   2 ☐   3 ☐

3 **Work with another student. Give your partner two pieces of advice about learning words from the same word family. Think about the form of the words and their pronunciation.**

a. _____

b. _____

For web resources relevant to this book, see:
www.englishforacademicstudy.com

These weblinks will provide you with further help in understanding the linguistic devices that lecturers use to help their audiences as well as help with key academic words in word families.

8   Digressions

In this unit you will:

- look at examples of digressions in lectures
- examine how lecturers sometimes mark the digressions
- practise following the lecturer's main points
- practise note-taking
- learn a number of expressions commonly used in lectures

| Task 1 | **Reasons for digressions** |

In Unit 7 we looked at ways of organizing information. However, even where lecturers organize their information well, and explicitly, they often move away from the main topic for a short time before returning to it. These are called **digressions**. There are a number of reasons why lecturers might digress during their lectures:

- to give a short definition of a new technical term
- to give a reference to a book on the topic
- to comment on events happening outside the lecture
- to comment on the point they are making
- to give general information about the course
- to give a personal **anecdote** to **illustrate** a point

1.1   **Think about your own experience of listening to lectures. Discuss the following questions in small groups.**

1. Can you think of any examples of digressions you have heard?
2. Do you think digressions are useful or confusing?
3. Can you think of any signposting words or phrases that lecturers use to signal the beginning or end of a digression?

> **Sound advice:**
> When lecturers make digressions, these create problems for listeners. You have to:
> - recognize that there is a digression
> - decide whether it is important to make a note or not
> - recognize when the lecturer has returned to the main point

Task 2 · Identifying digressions

You will read the transcript of a digression from the lecture on linguistics in Unit 6. The speaker is talking about the problem of embedded words.

2.1 Read the text, including the highlighted digression, and answer the questions below.

> The research that I've been involved in has been looking at factors responsible for our being able to cope successfully with this problem of embedded words, the fact that we're not constantly going off in the wrong direction being fooled by the sounds into hearing something that isn't there. Let's just try to think about what factors might be helping us not to go wrong. I've got three possible hypotheses here ==and again these are in the handout that I'll be giving you and you don't need to write these down, you'll get this text later on==. OK, the question is then, how are we successful most of the time in deciding where word boundaries come?

1. Why does the lecturer digress? Choose one of the reasons from Task 1.
2. How do you think the lecturer's delivery might change as she digresses?
   a. Do you think she would speak:
      1 more slowly, **2** more quickly, **3** at the same speed?
   b. Do you think she would speak:
      1 more quietly, **2** more loudly, **3** at the same level?
   c. Do you think she would pause:
      1 before the digression, **2** after the digression, **3** before and after?
   d. How do you think she would say the word *OK*?

2.2 ▶ **CD2: 12** Here is a digression from the lecture on social learning in Unit 7. Listen and read the extract. Then answer the questions.

1. What digression does the lecturer make and why?
2. How does she mark the beginning and end of digressions? Think about the questions relating to the lecturer's delivery after the digression in Ex 2.1.

> My first set of examples come from a – and I'm going to talk about some fairly classic experiments in this lecture, but I would point out before I go on that there is a really excellent chapter on this subject in Shettleworth's book, which is referred to in the reference list for this lecture. Sara Shettleworth has a superb chapter on social learning. It's called 'Learning from others'. It's very up-to-date, very thoughtful, very comprehensive, and I'm just going to mention just a few of the examples that she mentions. But if you seriously want to think about this area, and it involves many complexities, her chapter is a very good place to go. Anyway, some of the best-known work on social learning, or putative social learning, in rats, in animals, are about food preferences. These are examples of learning the significance of stimuli, learning what foods are good to eat and what foods are bad to eat.

In the next lecture the speaker is talking about how to design questionnaires. You heard part of this lecture in Unit 4, Ex 4.3. In this extract he is talking about issues to do with writing good questionnaires.

3.1 ▶ **CD2: 13 Listen to Part 1 and make notes on the main points of the lecture.**

_____

_____

_____

_____

_____

_____

_____

_____

_____

_____

3.2 **Compare your notes with another student then discuss the following questions.**
1. Did you understand the main points the lecturer made?
2. Did you make any notes on his digression?
3. Did you recognize when he started digressing? Finished digressing?

3.3 ▶ **CD2: 13 Listen again and pay attention to the digression. Answer the following questions with your partner.**
1. Why does the lecturer digress? Look back at the reasons in Task 1.
2. What exactly will students be required to do in their assessment?
3. What will they not do?
4. Why might the current students think they have to design a questionnaire?
5. Why has the lecturer changed the assessment from last year?
6. How did you recognize the beginning and the end of the digression?

3.4 ▶ **CD2: 13 Listen again and read the transcript on pages 91–92. How does the lecturer mark the beginning and end of the digression? Does the lecturer alter their delivery in any of the ways described in Ex 2.1?**

Task 4   Practice: Questionnaire design (2)

In Part 2 of the lecture on questionnaire design, the lecturer is discussing what researchers should do before they carry out market research using questionnaires.

4.1   Before you listen, discuss this situation in small groups.

> Groups of students at a university language centre have to carry out a survey on British people's attitudes to different aspects of life in the UK. In order to do this they have to prepare a questionnaire. Their lecturer gives them a list of things they should do and should not do in carrying out this survey.

As a group, prepare a list of dos and don'ts you think the lecturer gave the students.

4.2   ▶ CD2: 14 Listen to Part 2 and answer the following questions. Then compare your answers with your group.

1. What kind of objectives should students set?

   _____

2. Complete the information students should give.

   a. how they will collect the data

   b. _____

   c. how they will word the questions

   d. _____

3. When do students need the approval of the Ethics Committee?

   _____

4. What instruction were students given about how they should carry out the survey?

   _____

5. What topic did one group choose?

   _____

6. What mistake did the students make?

   _____

7. What mistake had the lecturer made?

   _____

8. Why should students pre-test the questionnaire?

   _____

9. What kind of information might students get from pre-testing (piloting)? Complete the gaps below with one to four words in each space.

   a. problems with the _____ of the questionnaire

   b. _____ questions

   c. whether questions are _____

4.3 Look at your answers from Ex 4.2 again. Which questions refer to the digression? Why do you think the lecturer made this digression?

4.4 ▶ **CD2: 14 Listen again and read the transcript on page 92. How does the lecturer mark the beginning and end of the digression? Was this done in the same way as in Task 3?**

Task 5	Practice: Integrated rural development

You are going to hear an extract from a lecture on the history of development economics. You heard part of this lecture in Unit 4, Ex 3.2. The speaker is talking about a development programme known as integrated rural development (IRD).

5.1 **Before you listen, look at the list of activities below. Which of these activities do you think would help rural development?**
1. Introducing new varieties of rice
2. Combating malaria
3. Cleaning up the water supply
4. Building new roads
5. Teaching adults to read
6. Sending foreign experts on short-term contracts
7. Providing Land Rovers
8. Documenting how the donors' money is spent

Compare your ideas with another student.

Image courtesy of Mott MacDonald Group Limited

5.2 ▶ **CD2: 15 Listen to the extract. Which of the activities in Ex 5.1 did the lecturer mention? Would you like to change your answers to the question in Ex 5.1? Compare with your partner.**

5.3   ▶ **CD2: 15 Listen again and answer the following questions. Compare your answers with your partner.**

1. What was the basic idea of IRD?

   _____

2. Why did the project organizers introduce measures to combat malaria and clean up the water?

   _____

3. What is the effect of building new roads?

   _____

4. How might adult literacy help?

   _____

5. What was good about the IRD programme?

   _____

6. Why was IRD not implemented in all parts of Kenya?

   _____

7. The speaker says the programme was a success, but qualifies the success. What was the problem with the programme?

   _____

8. What did the speaker find in his office?

   _____

9. What did he do with the documents?

   _____

10. What did the speaker think when he looked at the documents?

    _____

5.4   **Look at your answers to the questions in Ex 5.3. Write the question number beside the point it corresponds with.**

1. Commenting on the IRD programme _____
2. Giving an extended example of how IRD might work in practice _____
3. Explaining the rationale behind IRD _____
4. Digressing _____
5. Drawing a conclusion _____

Compare your answers with your partner.

5.5   **Discuss the digression with your partner. How is it relevant to the IRD programme?**

5.6   ▶ **CD2: 15** **Listen again and read the transcript on pages 92–93. What do the phrases in the box mean?**

Compare your ideas with your partner.

What on Earth?	on the grounds	increase their yields
give you synergy	that complements the agricultural measures	
my goodness	more than the sum of the parts	
it all went in the skip	with the benefit of hindsight	
a package of assistance	a scale-neutral technology	

Which of the phrases in the box do you think are:
1. used in spoken English only?
2. used in both spoken and written English?
3. useful to you in your degree subject?
4. useful to you in everyday English?

Compare your ideas with your partner.

Task 6	Microskills: Common expressions in lectures

In this activity, you will practise note-taking from short lecture extracts. In addition, you will focus on a number of expressions that commonly occur in lectures.

6.1   ▶ **CD2: 16** **This extract is from a lecture on politics. The lecturer is discussing the issue of whether states are free to act as they please, or whether there are <u>constraints</u> on the way they act. Listen and complete the notes.**

States can't _____ themselves from the outside world.

Growth of _____ states can't _____ what is going on around them. _____ has become more important, and states must respond. Strict appl. of _____ is being eroded.

6.2   ▶ **CD2: 16 Listen again and complete the extract with one to four words in each space.**

> I think that realism excludes the possibility – and it's a growing one – that states can simply isolate themselves from the outside world. The growth of television, the growth of mass communications, have meant that it's virtually impossible for states to ignore what's going on around them, and public opinion has become more important _____ within states, forcing states to do things that they might not otherwise do. So the strict application of power _____ _____ maintaining the hierarchy, of ignoring the interests of others, is simply slowly being withered away.

Discuss what the expressions in the spaces mean with another student.

6.3   ▶ **CD2: 17 This extract is from a lecture on office design. Listen and complete the notes.**

> Scand. ideas impact on Br. office design, e.g., factors influencing unusual design
>
> of the offices: _____
>
> _____

6.4   ▶ **CD2: 17 Listen again and complete the extract with one to four words in each space.**

> … ten years later, therefore, we have the Scandinavian ideas impacting on British office design. Another illustration of that might be, you'll discover in _____ _____ the lecture, that some of the factors which are driving the unusual, sometimes, configuration of office buildings on the Continent, not always but sometimes, are _____ employment legislation – workers' councils, employers' rights, employees' rights.

Discuss what the expressions in the spaces mean with your partner.

6.5 ▶ **CD2: 18 Extract 3 is from a lecture on the history of development economics. The lecturer is discussing the impact of the 1982 debt crisis on financial assistance to developing countries. Listen and complete the notes.**

1982–1992: _____ did not lend money to

dev.ing world. Only lenders were:

      – other governments

      – _____

      – multilateral agencies, e.g., _____

6.6 ▶ **CD2: 18 Listen again and complete the extract with one to four words in each space.**

Nineteen eighty-two. None of the commercial banks gave any money to the developing world for _____ ten years after the '82 debt crisis. They got such a bad fright by the debt crisis they _____ _____ ceased lending to the developing world. So the only people who were lending money to governments in the developing world from 1982 onwards were other governments, other aid agencies and other multilateral agencies like the IMF and the World Bank.

Discuss what the expressions in the spaces mean with your partner.

Unit summary

In this unit you have discussed why lecturers sometimes mark digressions and looked at examples of the digressions they make. You have practised following the lecturer's main points. You have also seen a number of expressions commonly used in lectures.

1 **Complete this summary with some of the words and phrases from the box.**

reference	main point	success	comment	recognize
explain	management	emphasize	anecdote	background

Even when lecturers organize their lectures well, they will sometimes digress from the main point. This might be to _____ further on the point they are making or in order to give a _____ to a book on the topic. They might want to give you some information about the course you are studying or say something about the _____ of the lecture they are giving at that moment. Lecturers will often tell students a personal _____ to illustrate a point they are making. When lecturers make digressions, it can create problems for listeners. To start with, you will need to _____ that there is a digression. Then you will need to decide whether the digression is important and whether you need to continue taking notes. Finally, you need to know when the lecturer has returned to the _____.

2 **Write one word or phrase that a lecturer might use to indicate that he/she is about to digress, and another he/she might use to indicate that he/she is returning to the main point.**

_____   _____

3 **You want to give some advice to a classmate about words and phrases that lecturers commonly use in lectures. Write six examples of expressions in the spaces below.**

_____   _____

_____   _____

_____   _____

For web resources relevant to this book, see:
www.englishforacademicstudy.com

These weblinks will provide you with further practice in following lectures containing digressions, as well as summarizing some of the skills you have learnt.

Glossary

abbreviation
A shortened form of a word or phrase, often used in notes or spoken English to save time, e.g., *UN* is an abbreviation of *United Nations*.

Academic Word List
A list of some of the most wide-ranging and frequently used English words used in academic contexts. Students can use the AWL to find the most useful academic words that they need to know when they study at an English-speaking university.

anecdote
A short account of an incident that is amusing or interesting.

approach (to a subject)
A way of thinking about or dealing with something. An approach is less clearly defined or strict than a method.

authentic
Authentic texts are texts from the real world, e.g., listening to the BBC News is an example of authentic listening practice, rather than listening to a text designed especially for a language learner.

background noise
Sound that is not what you want to listen to and may prevent you from listening effectively to something else, e.g., if you are listening to someone talking to you in the street, you may find it difficult because of the background noise from the traffic.

constraint
Something that limits what you are doing or want to do, e.g., there may be constraints of time, age or language.

content word
A word that carries meaning – usually a noun, verb, and sometimes an adjective or adverb, e.g., the content words are underlined in the following sentence: *My family is large*.

digress/digression
To move away from/a movement away from the main point you are talking or writing about. Speakers sometimes digress when they are giving a lecture (often to tell a short story or personal anecdote) and then return to the central topic.

embedded word
A word that appears to form part of a longer word, e.g., *cap* in *captain*. Embedded words may be confusing for learners because they may have no connection with the topic under discussion.

excerpt
A short extract or part of a recording or written text.

function word
A word that connects content words grammatically, but has little or no meaning by itself. Examples include articles, prepositions and conjunctions, e.g., the function words are underlined in the following sentence: *My family is large*.

illustrate
To clarify using examples, comparisons or visual images.

issue
A problem, topic or area for discussion or that needs to be worked on.

linear notes
Notes that are arranged so that the ideas are set out one after the other. The writer starts at the top of the page and works down to the bottom.

macroskills
Larger, more generalized skills that may consist of several different smaller skills (or sub-skills) that are used together. Listening is often referred to as a macroskill itself, but it also involves the macroskills of predicting and using background knowledge, recognizing how a lecture is structured, note-taking, etc.

microskills
Skills that enable the learner to piece together small pieces of information to build a bigger picture and make sense of something. Listening microskills include hearing which words are stressed or not stressed, recognizing where words begin and end in a stream of speech, etc.

mind map
A diagram used to represent words, ideas, tasks or other items linked to and arranged radially around a central key word or idea.

preview
A short introduction or overview that gives an idea of what is going to happen in a lecture, film or text.

scope
The area covered by an activity or subject, e.g., *A lecturer needs to limit the scope of a lecture.*

signal
The means by which a message is transmitted to others. This is usually through gesture; however, a signal can also be transmitted by specific words and phrases.

signpost(s)
Functional word(s) and/or phrase(s) that help to structure a spoken or written text and show the listener or reader where the speaker is going. For example, forward signposts may refer to what the speaker or writer is going to say next, e.g., *First I want to … then … finally …*

stress
Word stress is the way in which one syllable in a word is given more force. Stressed syllables are louder and longer than unstressed syllables. English places stress on key words or new information in a sentence, so students need to learn to recognize stressed words.

stress pattern
The way that syllables are stressed or unstressed in a word, or words are stressed or unstressed in an utterance. The stress patterns of words may be different within a word family, e.g., *finance* but *financial.*

syllable
A beat in a word. Each syllable has a vowel at its centre and consonants may surround the vowel. It is also possible to have a syllable with just a vowel. For example, the word *any* has two syllables (*a-ny*).

terminology
Vocabulary (or terms) used in a particular field, topic or area of study. These may be technical words or terms to describe complex concepts that are specific to that topic.

utterance
Something that one person says at a particular time. It could be a single word, a sentence or a longer stretch of speech.

weak form
Single-syllable function words when not stressed in speech often have a different pronunciation or appear as weak forms in English. The full vowel sound is normally replaced by the schwa /ə/ sound, e.g., *I can* /kən/ *do it* (weak form), *Yes, I can* /kæn/ (strong form).

word boundary
The place where one word ends and another word begins. There are not always clear word boundaries in rapid connected speech because speakers normally run words together and change or drop sounds, particularly where words begin or end with a vowel sound, e.g., in the utterance: *I got up at eight o'clock* there may be no clear word boundaries.

word family
A group of words that are closely related to each other because they share a common root or because they have related meanings, e.g., *family, familiar, familiarize, familiarization.*

These tracks are also available as video resources on the *EAS: Listening* DVD.

Unit 1: Listening and lectures

CD1 Track 1

Ex 2.2

Listen to Part 1 of a talk in which a lecturer describes some of the problems of listening. Then answer the following questions.

Part 1

Many students find listening to and understanding spoken English particularly difficult, and I think there are a number of reasons for this.

Firstly, there's the speed at which people talk. Obviously, when people are speaking quickly it's more difficult to understand them.

And then there's the issue of the topic that people are talking about. A topic you don't know much about is more difficult to understand than one you're familiar with. When you're listening to a familiar topic, you only need to concentrate on the new information, whereas if it's a new topic you often have to concentrate on just about everything.

There's also the problem of specialized vocabulary. There may be words you don't know. Now, if there's only a few words like this, people can generally follow the meaning, but if there are key words, or if there are a lot of unfamiliar words, then this can cause problems.

But there are two additional problems you may be faced with if English is not your first language.

When you're reading, you can see when one word ends and another one begins, because there's a space between them. But when you're listening, you can't. You often can't hear when one word ends and another begins, so you have to pick out the words you recognize and, from your understanding of the meaning, the context and your knowledge of English grammar, fill in the gaps.

When students learn English, they're generally reading texts rather than listening to them, so they get used to the written forms of words rather than the spoken forms. But when they learn these words, they build up in their mind an expectation of their pronunciation. And when they actually hear these words in natural speech, they often fail to recognize the words, because they're pronounced in an unexpected way.

So, there are two problems; firstly, it's difficult for students to know when one word ends and another begins, and secondly, they often fail to recognize words which they know in the written form.

CD1 Track 2

Ex 2.3

Now listen to Part 2 of the talk. The lecturer asks you to write down a phrase. Do this as you listen.

Part 2

So let's look at an example of this. I said earlier that students often fail to recognize words that they hear in natural speech. OK, so let's take the second part of that sentence, 'words they hear in natural speech'. Yeah? Now I'd like you to take a pen and a piece of paper and if you could write that bit of the sentence down for me please. Just 'words they hear in natural speech'. That part. OK? So you're writing down 'words they hear in natural speech'. OK, so how many words are there in that phrase? Are there three? Four? Five? In fact there are six. 'Words they hear in natural speech.' Now when I said this at normal speed, you may have heard 'hearinnatural' as one word, rather than three. And you may not have even recognized the word 'natural', because you had an expectation that it might be pronounced /ˈnætʃuræl/ or /ˈneɪtʃurəl/, instead of /ˈnætʃrəl/, which is how it is pronounced. You might have even heard the word *actual* or *national* instead of *natural*. But the point is, if you saw this phrase written down, you would probably understand the meaning, but when you hear it, it's more difficult for you to understand.

CD1 Track 3

Ex 2.4

Listen to Part 3 of the talk. Complete this excerpt by writing two to six words in each space.

Part 3

So what is the solution to these two problems? Well, firstly, you need to get as much practice listening to natural speech as possible. Listen to extracts from lectures and try to develop your understanding of how words and phrases are really pronounced, not how you expect them to be pronounced. And secondly, you need to accept that when you listen you may misunderstand what is being said. So you need to be ready to change your mind about your understanding of the meaning, if what you hear doesn't make sense compared to what you understood before. And this means taking a flexible, open-minded approach to listening.

CD1 Track 4

Ex 3.2

Listen to Part 1 of the talk and make notes about points 1–3.

Part 1

Good morning. I'm talking to you this morning because I'm interested in the differences between academic cultures in China and the UK. Now, what I mean by 'academic cultures' is simply how students study in the two countries – what are the different components of their courses, what teachers expect from them, and so on. And I'd like to present my ideas to you today and get some feedback from you. The thing I want to focus on particularly is lectures. I'm interested in the difference between lectures, both in terms of how the lectures are organized or presented and also in terms of how the lecture fits into the overall academic programme.

Now, the first question I need to address is, 'How do I know anything about lectures in China?' because I haven't studied there and in fact I haven't even been there. Well, I found out by interviewing Chinese students. What I did was conduct a so-called 'tracking study'. That means that you follow students over a period of time. What I did was to follow 12 Chinese students, all doing different courses, different master's courses at the University of Reading, and over their year of study I interviewed them three times individually. I interviewed them once

in the autumn term, once in the spring term and then again in the summer term. And the interviews lasted for about an hour, an hour and a quarter. I asked them a number of questions about studies in the UK and about their studies in China. So my information comes from them and so I have to say right from the beginning that I am talking here about information I got from 12 students, which is obviously a very small sample, and I don't know how representative what they said is of the Chinese education system as a whole. So we have to remember that limitation. I did choose different students from different parts of China, and I made sure that there was an equal number of men and women, and they were all studying different courses here at Reading, so there was a range of backgrounds and experience. But there is that limitation. However, I felt that what I was hearing from the students was actually very similar. I mean, what they were saying individually was more or less the same. So I felt that maybe there is some basis for what they said, and maybe what they did say and maybe their experience was not untypical, in general, of students in China.

CD1 Track 5

Ex 3.4

In Part 2 of the talk, the lecturer first talks about some of the characteristics of lectures in China and then compares these with lectures in the UK. Listen and make notes on the main points he makes.

Part 2

OK, so what did I find out? I think the first thing to say is that my impression is that in China the lecture delivers a lot of the content of the course, or the lecturer delivers a lot of the content of the course. And this seems to be especially true at undergraduate level. And just to reinforce this, the students I talked to were postgraduate students. In other words, they'd done undergraduate studies in China. I'm not sure about postgraduate studies in China. But what they said about undergraduate courses was that a lot of the course content came through the lectures. In other words, the students go to the lectures, they make notes in the lectures, and at the end of the term, or at the end of the year, if they have a test or examination, in many cases they simply give back to the lecturer what the lecturer gave to them during the lectures. And that seems to be sufficient to pass the exam and pass the course.

So, the lecture is the important vehicle of the course content; it carries the course content.

Now, the second point they made about lectures was that in China they don't seem to be very interactive, in the sense that students sit, they listen, they make lots and lots of notes. But they don't often ask questions during the lecture or at the end of the lecture, and they don't have much discussion, either during or at the end of the lecture, and that is not expected of them. So they really, in China, lectures don't seem to be very interactive.

Another point which students made to me, which I thought was interesting, was that the main points, the important points of a lecture, are often explicitly marked by the lecturer. The lecturer might say, 'OK, this point is very important, make a note of this' and might even write things on the blackboard, which the students would copy down verbatim. In other words, they would copy down exactly what he was writing. So this was interesting, it seems that the students don't have to decide for themselves what is important, what is less important. The lecturer tells them. Now obviously that's a very general and very rough caricature of what students told me about Chinese lectures. But how does that compare with the UK situation?

Well, in the UK, I think it's fair to say that the course content is not only delivered through the lectures. If you study on a UK course and if you only give back to the lecturer in examinations, or tests, or assignments or essays, if you only give back what he or she says during the lecture, then I don't think you are going to pass the exam, the course. I think what lecturers are doing in the UK is something different. I think either they are giving an overview of the main ideas connected with the subject, or they are giving some general background to the subject, and then it's the student's responsibility to go away, and to do lots of reading, and to really fill in the details, and to fully understand the theories, the ideas the lecturer is talking about.

And that really brings me to the point of reading. Because what I understood from my Chinese students was that in China, certainly at undergraduate level, they had one course book for each course, and just to emphasize that, they seemed to have one course book. And there was a very close correspondence between what the lecturer was saying and what was in the course book. In other words, if the students wanted to, they could go away at the end of the lecture and

read the course book, and it would essentially say what the lecturer himself had said, so there was that kind of reinforcement. In the UK it's very different. There's not one course book for one course. You can't just go away and read one book, and find the entire content of the lectures there. You will have to read a lot of books and a lot of articles to fill in what the lecturer has given you. So in the UK, reading, and reading really widely, is an essential part of what students do after lectures. In China it seems that there is a lot less reading, and the reading is mainly concentrated on this one course book.

That's one thing about the UK. The other thing about the UK, the UK lecture, is that lecturers here do expect students to interact, to ask questions, to raise points of view, to make comments, to enter into discussion. Now obviously how much discussion there is, how much interaction there is, depends very much on how many students there are in the lecture. Here at Reading, in some cases, we may have 20 students in a lecture and on other courses you may have 200 students in a lecture, and obviously there's less discussion if there are more students. There's less time for questions. But interactiveness in general is very important in the UK.

Well, those are just some of my impressions of the differences between lectures in China and the UK, but I would really be very interested now in hearing your opinions – whether you think what I've talked about is true from your experience or not.

Unit 2: Introductions to lectures

CD1 Track 6
Ex 1.4

Listen to the introduction. Then answer the questions.

Migration
There has been a lot of talk recently in the newspapers and on television about immigration to the UK from countries joining the EU, countries like Poland, and more recently Romania and Bulgaria. This discussion is centred on questions like whether this is good for the British economy or not – in terms of productivity, or impact on national infrastructure, for example, on the health and education services, etc. However, that's not the type of migration that I want to look at today. What I want to look at is internal migration, i.e., the movement of people from country to city, and vice versa, and from one city to another.

CD1 Track 7

Ex 3.2

Listen to the introduction to the lecture *Britain and the European Monetary Union*. Which functions from the checklist in Task 2 does the lecturer use?

Britain and the European Monetary Union
OK, good morning. Well, first up, can you all hear me? Good. Well that's a good place to start. Well, today I'm going to be talking to you mainly about Britain and the so-called Eurozone, the European Monetary Union. As I am sure you know there are currently, although this may have changed by the time you listen to the recording of this lecture, 17 countries in the Eurozone; the last country to join being Estonia in 2011. You also know, as you are living in the UK and are using British currency (pounds and pence) on a daily basis, that Britain decided not to join the Eurozone, and given the problems the euro has had over the last few years, and is still having, many British people consider that to have been the right decision. Incidentally, the UK is not alone in this, as other EU countries also opted out, for example, Denmark. I'll come back to the reasons the UK did not originally join later in this lecture.

Now I have already talked in previous lectures about the early history of the European Union, or the European Economic Community, as it was originally known. I also talked about the reasons Britain was reluctant to join the EEC, and why some other members of the EEC, France in particular, were not convinced that Britain should join either. One of the main reasons for this was, I suggested, that Britain felt it had a special arrangement with the United States and with its former colonies in the Commonwealth and didn't want to endanger this relationship by joining. And after Britain's participation in the wars with Iraq, you might conclude that the British still believe they have a special relationship with the US – even if the US may not see this in the same way.

However, leaving all that aside, today I want to talk about three things. Firstly, I am going to talk about the process of how the euro was introduced, and then I'm going to talk about the economic and political tests that a new country has to pass in order to join the euro – despite the problems in the Eurozone there are still countries that would like to join. However, as the title of my lecture suggests, I am going to spend most of the time today talking about why Britain did not adopt the euro, and what that said, and still says, about Britain's attitude in general to membership of the European Union.

CD1 Track 8

Ex 3.4

Listen to the introduction to the lecture *Globalization*. Which functions from the checklist in Task 2 does the lecturer use?

Globalization
Globalization is a term that you hear everywhere these days, whether people are talking about food – McDonald's and other fast-food companies in particular – or about the economy, with more and more multinational companies all over the world, or about information, with the Internet and the spread of the English language making the same information available at the same time to people all over the world. Arguably, globalization also includes national cultures, with some authorities suggesting, as I myself do in my latest book, that national cultures as we knew them no longer exist. In any case, globalization is often said to be the single most profound and wide-ranging change in human history. Ever. Well, that is something that you can discuss later – you may have your own opinions on whether this is true or not. But it does go without saying that it is something which affects everybody's life; it affects people as diverse as farmers in the Third World, stockbrokers in London and New York, or global tycoons in multimillion-dollar empire industries. So, obviously, there is something in which a political scientist, or, for that matter, an historian, or a sociologist, or a geographer, or a whole range of other disciplines, might well be interested.

What I'm going to try to do today is give you some understanding of the history of globalization, what globalization means to people on a local level and what its implications could be for the whole world.

So I'm going to be talking on a global scale – which is appropriate for this topic – and I'm also going to be covering some fairly long periods of time.

CD1 Track 9

Ex 3.6

Listen to the introduction to the lecture *Magistrates' courts*. Which functions from the checklist in Task 2 does the lecturer use?

Magistrates' courts

Good morning, everybody. In spite of what John just said, I'm not going to spend a lot of time talking about the family work. That's a specialist area of the Magistrates' court. As John says, it deals with non-criminal matters involving the state and children. So, for example, in the case of family break-up, it would involve making parental contact orders where the parents can't agree on how much contact time each parent should have with the child – after divorce, for example. It also deals with parental responsibility. So that means fathers who are refusing to pay for the maintenance of their children. Then, finally, it deals with any kind of case involving the state and the child – notably, when the state wishes to take the child from the care of the parents and put it in the care of somebody else or in the care of the local authority, the government, and also when the child is to be adopted by another family. But that is another specialist area. What we are mainly concerned with today is the criminal court, and that is what I am going to spend most of my time talking about this morning.

So this is a court – the Magistrates' court deals only with offences, criminal offences. So we're not dealing, for example, with disputes between neighbours. For example, if you have an argument with your neighbour about the noise that is being made, or the height of his hedge which is preventing the light getting into your garden – all those kinds of things are dealt with in the civil court, but here we are dealing with the criminal court, so it's crimes against the state as defined by the legal code. So I just want to make that clear from the beginning.

So within that criminal justice system, first of all we are dealing with England and Wales here. There is a slightly different system that operates in Scotland – so we're talking about England and Wales only. Within that justice system there are two main courts. One is the crown court which deals with very serious offences. So those would be the ones that you've probably all seen on television where there's a judge and 12 members of a jury. Those are only for serious offences. We are dealing with the lesser offences and those are dealt with in the courts that I'm going to talk to you about today, and that is the Magistrates' court.

CD1 Track 10

Ex 4.1

Listen and complete the sentence from the introduction to *Britain and the European Monetary Union*.

However, as the title of my lecture suggests, I am going to spend most of the time today talking about why Britain did not adopt the euro, and what that said, and still says, about Britain's attitude in general to membership of the European Union.

CD1 Track 11

Ex 4.2

Listen and complete the following sentences from the introduction to *Magistrates' courts*. Write one word in each space.

So, for example, in the case of family break-up, it would involve making parental contact orders where the parents can't agree on how much contact time each parent should have with the child …

What we are mainly concerned with today is the criminal court, and that is what I am going to spend most of my time talking about this morning.

CD1 Track 12

Ex 4.4

Listen to a recording about security and computers. Complete the text with one word in each space.

Security is an important aspect of using a computer that many people do not pay much attention to. If you buy a laptop or personal computer, you will probably want to connect to the Internet. If so, it is important that you install security software which will protect it from attack by viruses or spyware. Now there is a wide range of products available on the market which are relatively cheap and which provide a variety of different features. For example, in addition to checking their computer for viruses, parents can use the software to control which websites their children can access. You should not assume, however, that you are 100% safe if you are using such security software. You should make sure that you have backup copies of your work, and you should be very careful about keeping important information, such as bank account details, on your computer.

CD1 Track 13
Ex 4.5

Listen to a recording about competition between large supermarket chains and small local shops. Complete the text with one word in each space.

Because of planning restrictions, the large UK supermarket chains are looking to expand their businesses and increase profits by opening smaller 'convenience stores'. Organizations representing small, independent shops protest that they now face unfair competition from the large chains. And they accuse the large chains of a number of practices that make it difficult for them to compete. Firstly, it is alleged that below-cost pricing is used by large supermarkets to force smaller, local shops out of business. Secondly, the large chains often buy up land which is not immediately used, and this prevents smaller local businesses from entering the market.

There is also some concern that the large chains are treating their suppliers unfairly. Farmers claim that they are being paid less for their products, and they are reluctant to complain for fear of losing key contracts.

However, supermarkets argue that the consumer is the best regulator of the market.

CD1 Track 14
Ex 4.7

Listen to a recording about the effect of global warming on numbers of polar bears. Complete the text with one word in each space.

Wildlife experts predict that numbers of polar bears will decline by at least 50% over the next 50 years because of global warming. Polar bears rely on sea ice to catch seals for food, and it has emerged that ice floes in the Arctic are disappearing at an alarming rate. Now scientists report that the animals are already beginning to suffer the effects of climate change in some parts of Canada, and if there is any further delay in tackling this problem, polar bears may be extinct by the end of the century.

CD1 Track 15
Ex 4.8

Listen to a recording about monitoring water levels in rivers. Complete the text with one word in each space.

Scientists are now able to monitor river levels using information from satellites by using a computer programme devised by researchers at De Montfort University in Leicester. Satellites have been able to measure the height of the sea by timing how long it takes to receive a beam bounced back off waves. But, until now, interference from objects on the banks of rivers has made it impossible to measure river levels.

However, the new programme, which is based on data collected over the last decade, is specially designed to filter out this interference. This new technology will be particularly useful in monitoring river-levels in remote areas. It will, for example, enable scientists to examine river level patterns over the entire Amazon River basin, contributing towards our understandings of climate change.

Unit 3: Identifying key ideas in lectures

CD1 Track 16
Ex 2.2

Listen to Part 1 of the lecture, which is in three sections. Identify the three sections and number them in the correct order.

Franchising
Part 1
Section 1
The form of business development I'm going to look at now is franchising. The term 'franchising' covers a wide range of business arrangements, but today I'm going to focus on 'business format franchising'.

If you own a small or medium-sized enterprise, you may reach a stage in its development at which, in order to develop further, you need large amounts of capital, or you need to reorganize your business, or to bring into the management team new skills. Well, let's say you own four or five hairdressing salons in your city which are very profitable. You want to expand the business, but recognize firstly that a lot more money will need to be invested, and secondly that you will not be able to exert the same amount of personal control over the day-to-day running of the business that you've been used to. This stage in the growth of the business may present the entrepreneur with risks that he or she is unwilling to run. However, one way of minimizing such risks, while at the same time continuing to develop and profit from a successful brand, is by franchising your business.

Section 2

So, what is franchising? Well, here is a definition from the British Franchising Association website. And it says, 'Business format franchising is the granting of a licence by one person (the franchisor) to another (the franchisee), which entitles the franchisee to trade under the trademark/trade name of the franchisor and to make use of an entire package, comprising all the elements necessary to establish a previously untrained person in the business, and to run it with continual assistance on a predetermined basis.' This package would include things like training, consultancy arrangements, possibly supplies, marketing on a national scale, etc., etc.

Section 3

So, for example, if you own a group of successful fast-food restaurants trading under the same name, you may decide to run your business as a franchise. You would allow other businesspeople to open their own branches of the fast-food chain, using your trademark, and in fact you would probably supply a lot of the signage and materials necessary to maintain a uniform brand. In return, the franchisee pays you, the franchisor, an initial fee, that is to say a fee paid at the beginning of the business arrangement, and also an ongoing management service fee. This management service fee is related to the volume of business the franchisee is doing, so it might be calculated as a percentage of the turnover, or as a mark-up on supplies provided by the franchisor. So there are two kinds of fee: the one-off initial fee to set up the franchise, and the ongoing management service fee.

CD1 Track 17
Ex 2.3

Listen to Part 1, Section 1 again and answer the questions.

Section 1

The form of business development I'm going to look at now is franchising. The term 'franchising' covers a wide range of business arrangements, but today I'm going to focus on 'business format franchising'.

If you own a small or medium-sized enterprise, you may reach a stage in its development at which, in order to develop further, you need large amounts of capital, or you need to reorganize your business, or to bring into the management team new skills. Well, let's say you own four or five hairdressing salons in your city which are very profitable. You want to expand the business, but recognize firstly that a lot more money will need to be invested, and secondly that you will not be able to exert the same amount of personal control over the day-to-day running of the business that you've been used to. This stage in the growth of the business may present the entrepreneur with risks that he or she is unwilling to run. However, one way of minimizing such risks, while at the same time continuing to develop and profit from a successful brand, is by franchising your business.

CD1 Track 18
Ex 2.4

Listen to Part 1, Section 2 again and answer the following questions.

Section 2

So, what is franchising? Well, here is a definition from the British Franchising Association website. And it says, 'Business format franchising is the granting of a licence by one person (the franchisor) to another (the franchisee), which entitles the franchisee to trade under the trademark/trade name of the franchisor and to make use of an entire package, comprising all the elements necessary to establish a previously untrained person in the business, and to run it with continual assistance on a predetermined basis.' This package would include things like training, consultancy arrangements, possibly supplies, marketing on a national scale, etc., etc.

CD1 Track 19
Ex 2.5

Listen to Part 1, Section 3 again and answer the following questions.

Section 3

So, for example, if you own a group of successful fast-food restaurants trading under the same name, you may decide to run your business as a franchise. You would allow other businesspeople to open their own branches of the fast-food chain, using your trademark, and in fact you would probably supply a lot of the signage and materials necessary to maintain a uniform brand. In return, the franchisee pays you, the franchisor, an initial fee, that is to say a fee paid at the beginning of the business arrangement, and also an ongoing management service fee. This management service fee is related to the volume of business the franchisee is doing, so it might be calculated as a percentage of the turnover, or as a mark-up on supplies provided by the franchisor. So there are two kinds of fee: the one-off initial fee to set up the franchise, and the ongoing management service fee.

CD1 Track 20

Ex 3.2

Listen to Part 2 of the lecture.

Part 2
Section 1

There are a number of issues you need to consider when deciding whether or not to franchise your business. Firstly, there needs to be a relatively stable, long-term market for the product or service you are franchising. This is partially because substantial investment in time and money is required to set up and develop a franchise operation, and partly because you need an established market with potential for long-term growth to attract franchisees. So, something like a chain of hairdressing salons might offer potential for a franchise, because there will always be a demand for women to have their hair cut and styled. On the other hand, a franchise to promote and sell a new kind of children's toy might be less successful, because toys tend to have a short market lifespan.

Section 2

In addition – and this is fairly obvious – you will need a fairly wide margin between cost and income. Remember that the gross margin needs to provide a return on the investment to both the franchisor and the franchisee. So you will need to keep costs low and prices as high as the market will bear. One advantage of a franchise operation is that supplies can be bought in bulk across the whole franchise, which will help to keep costs down. But you can see that franchising would be unsuitable in a market where the margin between cost and income is very narrow.

Section 3

The franchisor will need to provide support and training to the franchisee because, in addition to the brand, what you are selling is a way of doing business that has proved successful. You will need to produce an operating manual that describes in detail all the different systems and procedures involved in the business, and the performance and quality standards, but you will also have to provide some kind of training for the franchisees and possibly his employees, certainly in setting up the operation and possibly on a regular, ongoing basis. The important point here is that for a franchise to be successful, it should be possible for the franchisee to develop the skills required to operate the business fairly quickly. So, although some initial training may be required, the franchisee should be able to operate the business efficiently and successfully within a few months of start-up. In some types of franchise, the skills required may be acquired quickly; in others, the franchisee may have already developed most of the necessary skills in previous employment. So, for example, someone operating a franchise in the restaurant industry is likely to have experience either as an employee in a restaurant, or in a similar field.

CD1 Track 21

Ex 3.4

Listen to Part 2, Section 1 again and answer the following questions.

Section 1

There are a number of issues you need to consider when deciding whether or not to franchise your business. Firstly, there needs to be a relatively stable, long-term market for the product or service you are franchising. This is partially because substantial investment in time and money is required to set up and develop a franchise operation, and partly because you need an established market with potential for long-term growth to attract franchisees. So, something like a chain of hairdressing salons might offer potential for a franchise, because there will always be a demand for women to have their hair cut and styled. On the other hand, a franchise to promote and sell a new kind of children's toy might be less successful, because toys tend to have a short market lifespan.

CD1 Track 22

Ex 3.5

Listen to Part 2, Section 2 again and answer the following questions.

Section 2

In addition – and this is fairly obvious – you will need a fairly wide margin between cost and income. Remember that the gross margin needs to provide a return on the investment to both the franchisor and the franchisee. So you will need to keep costs low and prices as high as the market will bear. One advantage of a franchise operation is that supplies can be bought in bulk across the whole franchise, which will help to keep costs down. But you can see that franchising would be unsuitable in a market where the margin between cost and income is very narrow.

CD1 Track 23
Ex 3.6

Listen to Part 2, Section 3 again and answer the following questions.

Section 3

The franchisor will need to provide support and training to the franchisee because, in addition to the brand, what you are selling is a way of doing business that has proved successful. You will need to produce an operating manual that describes in detail all the different systems and procedures involved in the business, and the performance and quality standards, but you will also have to provide some kind of training for the franchisees and possibly his employees, certainly in setting up the operation and possibly on a regular, ongoing basis. The important point here is that for a franchise to be successful, it should be possible for the franchisee to develop the skills required to operate the business fairly quickly. So, although some initial training may be required, the franchisee should be able to operate the business efficiently and successfully within a few months of start-up. In some types of franchise, the skills required may be acquired quickly; in others, the franchisee may have already developed most of the necessary skills in previous employment. So, for example, someone operating a franchise in the restaurant industry is likely to have experience either as an employee in a restaurant, or in a similar field.

CD1 Track 24
Ex 4.1

Listen to Part 3 of the lecture. Make notes on the key points in your notebook.

Part 3
Section 1

One further issue you may need to consider is whether the business is transferable to another geographical area. If you have developed your business serving one particular part of the country and you want to set up a franchise network covering a much larger area – the whole country, for example – another thing you will have to consider is whether there is a similar market for your product or service in different regions. It may be, for example, that competition in other parts of the country may be so strong that it is difficult for franchisees to survive, or that for localized socioeconomic or cultural reasons the business may not be as profitable.

Section 2

Finally, when you are setting up a franchise network, you will need to bear in mind that you will be losing direct control of the way your brand is perceived by the customer, so this brings me to my last point, which is to emphasize the importance of protecting your brand. I am sure you are all aware that it often takes a long time to establish a distinctive brand with a valuable reputation, but that this reputation can be damaged comparatively quickly if, for example, quality standards are not consistently applied. The detailed operating manual, that I referred to earlier, will play a role in maintaining the brand but, just as important, you need to take care selecting franchisees and monitoring their operations. In addition to checking that franchisees have the relevant skills and experience to run a successful business, you also need to ensure that they share the same business values as you, that they accept the importance of maintaining the brand and that they are clear about what they can or can't change about the way the business is run – so people who are very individualistic will probably not make good franchisees.

Section 3

The written agreement between the franchisor and franchisee should specify very clearly what performance and quality standards are expected, and much of the initial training will be ensuring that staff have the skills to achieve these standards. However, regular visits to franchise units are essential in ensuring that the standards are being applied consistently and uniformly, and ongoing training may be necessary to deal with issues that are uncovered in these visits. Protecting the brand is ultimately in the interests of both the franchisor and the franchisee because, for the franchisee, one of the main advantages in running a franchise is that they are buying into and helping to consolidate an established brand.

CD1 Track 25
Ex 4.2

Listen to Part 3, Section 1 again and complete the excerpt with one to three words in each space.

Section 1

One further issue you may need to consider is whether the business is transferable to another geographical area. If you have developed your business serving one particular part of the country and you want to set up a franchise network covering a much larger area – the whole country, for example – another thing you will have to consider is whether there is a similar market for your product or service in different regions. It may be, for example, that competition in other parts of the country may be so strong that it is difficult for franchisees to survive, or that for localized socioeconomic or cultural reasons the business may not be as profitable.

CD1 Track 26
Ex 4.3

Listen to Part 3, Section 2 again.

Section 2

Finally, when you are setting up a franchise network, you will need to bear in mind that you will be losing direct control of the way your brand is perceived by the customer, so this brings me to my last point, which is to emphasize the importance of protecting your brand. I am sure you are all aware that it often takes a long time to establish a distinctive brand with a valuable reputation, but that this reputation can be damaged comparatively quickly if, for example, quality standards are not consistently applied. The detailed operating manual that I referred to earlier will play a role in maintaining the brand but, just as important, you need to take care selecting franchisees and monitoring their operations. In addition to checking that franchisees have the relevant skills and experience to run a successful business, you also need to ensure that they share the same business values as you, that they accept the importance of maintaining the brand and that they are clear about what they can or can't change about the way the business is run – so people who are very individualistic will probably not make good franchisees.

CD1 Track 27
Ex 4.4

Listen to Part 3, Section 3 again and complete the notes in as much detail as you think is necessary.

Section 3

The written agreement between the franchisor and franchisee should specify very clearly what performance and quality standards are expected, and much of the initial training will be ensuring that staff have the skills to achieve these standards. However, regular visits to franchise units are essential in ensuring that the standards are being applied consistently and uniformly, and ongoing training may be necessary to deal with issues that are uncovered in these visits. Protecting the brand is ultimately in the interests of both the franchisor and the franchisee because, for the franchisee, one of the main advantages in running a franchise is that they are buying into and helping to consolidate an established brand.

CD1 Track 28
Ex 5.3

Listen to the sentences and write in the missing prefix to each word.

1. All trade unions were declared illegal by the government.
2. This is one example of a mismatch between the individual's goals and those of the organization.
3. They found no significant correlation between class size and levels of achievement.
4. Real estate transactions rose by 30% last month.
5. Prices are determined through the interaction of supply and demand.
6. These animals exhibited abnormal behaviour compared to the control group.

CD1 Track 29
Ex 5.4

Listen to the sentences and complete them with two to four words in each space.

1. We had to get the photos enlarged because the detail was not very clear on the original ones.
2. Many doctors work long, irregular hours, which put them under a lot of stress.

3. Crime prevention is an important aspect of the police's work, but it is often difficult to assess its effectiveness.

4. Doctors have noticed an increase in eating disorders, such as bulimia and anorexia, not just among young women but, surprisingly, among young men.

5. These plants should be grown in partial shade, rather than in direct sunlight.

6. Researchers have found that inexperienced drivers are much more likely to be involved in traffic accidents.

CD1 Track 30
Ex 5.5

Listen to the groups of sentences. Complete the sentences with two to four words in each space.

1. a. Children need a **secure** environment in which to grow up.
   b. Many immigrants are only able to find low-paid, insecure jobs.
   c. The money was invested in securities and property.

2. a. Achievement levels **vary** considerably from school to school in the city.
   b. Some economists believe that interest rates can be predicted by examining key economic variables.
   c. In the Eden Project they have managed to create a wide variety of habitats.
   d. There is significant variation in access to health care in different parts of the country.

3. a. How are we going to **solve** this problem?
   b. You need to dissolve the pesticide in water before applying it to the crop.
   c. There appears to be insoluble conflict between the two countries, despite years of peace negotiations.

4. a. A mass spectrometer was used to **analyze** the gases.
   b. Further analysis of the data is needed to confirm these initial findings.
   c. The course is designed to help students to develop their analytical skills.

5. a. The results **indicate** that the virus mutates more rapidly than was first believed.
   b. All the main economic indicators suggest that the economy is recovering.
   c. The strike was indicative of the level of the workers' frustration.

6. a. Chomsky was a fierce **critic** of Bush Senior's foreign policy.
   b. There was some criticism of the way the election had been administered.
   c. The negotiations were critical to the establishment of peace in the area.

Unit 4: Note-taking: Part 1

CD1 Track 31
Ex 2.2

Listen to the recording and read the extract from the transcript at the same time.

Britain's transport problems
Part 1

So Britain's roads, and especially those in the south-east, are overcrowded. There are too many cars on the roads, and at particular times of the day and in particular places, traffic is either very slow or at a standstill. Now, this has a number of effects. Firstly, there is the economic effect, all the time wasted in traffic jams, which means a loss of productivity. Then there's the environmental effect. Cars produce a lot of pollution, which damages the local environment, but it also contributes to global warming. And there's also an effect on people's health. In addition to the poor air quality and the damage this causes people's lungs, the stress of being stuck in traffic each day leads to higher risk of heart disease.

CD1 Track 32
Ex 2.5

Listen to Parts 2–5 of the lecture and make notes on page 34.

Part 2

So, how do we deal with this problem? It is widely accepted among researchers and policy makers that there isn't just one simple solution. For example, it's generally agreed that simply building more roads is not the solution, as research shows that this just leads to an increase in traffic and, in the long term, it worsens the problems I have just described. So, what is needed is a whole range of measures aimed at improving the transport system. The problem is that changes in transport policy take many years to plan and implement. Transport is a politically sensitive issue, so when governments change, then the policy often changes too. This makes it difficult to bring about major changes in policy.

CD1 Track 33
Part 3

Between 1997 and 2010, the Labour government in power at the time adopted an integrated transport policy. What we mean by integrated, is that different aspects of the transport system – so road, rail, air travel – are planned in relation to one another. One of the main issues addressed by that government was how to encourage car drivers to drive less, and to use public transport more. The first point is that just making improvements to the public transport system is not enough to get drivers to use buses or trains. We can provide more buses and trains so that these are less crowded, and we can make them cleaner, safer environments to travel in, and all this will need investment of course, but, even if we do all this, drivers will still prefer to use their cars.

CD1 Track 34
Part 4

So the Labour government tried a number of measures aimed at encouraging drivers to use public transport more. The government tried to encourage car-sharing, so, in some experimental projects on crowded roads, lanes have been designated for use by cars with more than one occupant; CCTV cameras are used to police the trials. The thinking is that if people believe that they can get to work more quickly by driving in this faster lane, then they are more likely to share cars.

In London, congestion charging has had some success; cars are charged to enter a central zone and again, CCTV cameras linked to a computer system are used to ensure compliance. This reduces the number of cars in the centre of London, and the income from congestion charging is then invested in London's public transport system. This is an example of what is meant by an integrated policy.

CD1 Track 35
Part 5

The problem with many of these schemes is that they put pressure on motorists, on drivers. Drivers have already felt under pressure because of the dramatic increases in fuel prices. When the coalition government came to power in 2010, it promised to 'end the war on the motorist'. It was less interested in the schemes to encourage people to drive less, so, for example, the congestion charge zone has been reduced in size. The coalition is more interested in projects to develop the rail network, including a high-speed rail line connecting the north and south of England, and in responding to the growth in air travel either by building a new airport or developing an existing one.

So this shows some of the difficulties involved in encouraging people to drive less and use public transport more, but to sum up the point I made earlier, a whole range of measures attacking the problem from different angles is more likely to be successful than one 'big idea'.

CD1 Track 36
Ex 3.2

In Part 1 of the extract, the lecturer is discussing the reasons for rapid economic growth in East Asia in the 1990s. Listen and continue the following notes.

The East Asian economic miracle
Part 1

And a lot of time was spent in the 1990s trying to interpret the so-called 'East Asian miracle'. There are big disputes about the extent to which the East Asian miracle shows that market liberalism works, particularly when you realize that one of these countries is China, with a highly controlled economy indeed. The Japanese have never run a purely free-market economy. Neither have the Koreans. On the other hand, Singapore, Hong Kong, were swashbuckling free-market capitalism. So there were debates about the extent to which state intervention in the free market pushed forward the East Asian miracle.

CD1 Track 37
Ex 3.3

In Part 2 of the extract, the lecturer goes on to discuss another factor. Listen to Part 2 and continue the notes.

Part 2

But nobody disagreed about one element of the East Asian miracle, and that was investment in people. Country after country in East Asia, it was argued, had undertaken reasonably equitable investments in health care, education and training of people in those countries. And it was argued that this was a major stimulus to industrialization in this area, that you could always hire a lot of people at low labour rates, but who were in reasonably good health, who were literate and who had reasonable skills.

And that was the difference between East Asia and, for example, Africa and Latin America. Or a difference, for that matter, between East Asia and South Asia.

CD1 Track 38

Ex 4.1

Listen to this extract from Track 37. The main stressed words in this sentence are marked in bold.

…, that you could **always** hire a lot of people at **low** labour rates, but who were in reasonably good **health**, who were **literate** and who had reasonable **skills**.

CD1 Track 39

Ex 4.2

Listen to the following sentence from Track 36.

The Japanese have never run a purely free-market economy. Neither have the Koreans.

CD1 Track 40

Ex 4.3

Listen to the extract and complete the sentences with two to seven words in each space.

You need to pre-test the questionnaire. This is really important. Those of you, some of you, will be doing this for, you know, your dissertation. Some of you, I know, are collecting primary data. You need to pre-test the thing, because you're the researcher. You're very close to the subject. You know what you're talking about, but you've got to check that other people do as well. And if you want a statistically valid sample of a hundred or two hundred people, then you've got to make sure that you're collecting the data properly. And it's here that these pre-tests, or pilots, they're going to tell you whether it's going to work or not.

So make sure that you do pilots and, you know, this can be, sort of, half a dozen different people that you question. I mean, you'll soon find out whether you've got any potential … or any doubts about the length of the questionnaire, or the style of particular questions, or whether the sort of questions that you're asking are valid. You'll soon find out from that. So, piloting or pre-testing is really important.

Unit 5: Note-taking: Part 2

CD1 Track 41

Ex 3.1

Listen to a lecturer talking about language learning. Continue the following notes.

Extract 1
Purposes of education

Three very broad perspectives from Littlewood, on the purposes of education. One is a very traditional one: to pass on value, knowledge and culture. So that you see education as passing from the previous generation down to the next generation – the knowledge they will need. Another purpose of education is to prepare learners as members of society. So you have needs which you feel your society must fulfil, and you view education as a vehicle for doing this. And that will influence how language is taught – we'll see how in a moment. And the third view, which is much more humanistic, a humanistic view of education, is where you see learners as individual selves who must be developed. And the process of education as being developing the self – bringing out the individual's best characteristics, allowing them to learn and to fulfil their potential.

CD1 Track 42

Ex 3.2

Listen and continue the following notes.

Extract 2
World economy

What you have to understand is that from the early 1970s onwards there was this primary boom and there were signs of inflation in the world economy. In 1971, America left the gold standard. The value of the dollar had been linked to the value of gold and suddenly the government decided to cut it free. It was effectively devalued. Remember, in 1970, the American economy made up about a third of the total product of the world economy. Today it's about 25% or even less than that, but then the dollar had an even greater influence on the world economy.

So, before the 1970s, we had fixed exchange rates, but from 1971, America devalued the dollar and the exchange rates floated. And from that moment onwards, the major industrial economies, which in the '50s and '60s had had inflation rates of 1%, 2%, 3% per year, suddenly found themselves with inflation rates running at 10%, 15%, 20%. None of you in this room will believe me, probably, when I tell you that, in 1971, Britain's inflation rate was 25%, yes. I can hardly believe that as the words come out of my mouth, and I can remember the year very, very distinctly.

CD1 Track 43
Ex 4.2

Listen to this extract from a lecture entitled *Health in the UK* and make notes.

Health in the UK

Ok, so we've looked at some of the problems in the developing world.

What I would like to do now is look at the health situation in the developed world, with particular reference to the United Kingdom. I think the situation can be summarized briefly like this: firstly, life expectancy – how long people are living – is increasing. Secondly, we are taking more and more drugs and as a result of this we are curing, or at least controlling, many illnesses. However, what we are not doing as well as we should is stopping people getting sick in the first place.

Let me just illustrate this point with some statistics.

I've said that life expectancy in the UK is increasing and that's true. For example, let's look at men aged between 35 and 74. The number of men in this age group who died dropped by 42% between 1990 and 2000. Now that's a huge fall. Forty-two per cent fewer deaths in this age group over a ten-year period. Now, it is clear to me that much of this fall has been due to the amount of drugs we take now to cure problems.

If we look at heart disease, for example, and the drugs we take to regulate or 'cure' it, we can see that the number of prescriptions issued by doctors has almost quadrupled – increased by just under 400% – in the last 20 years. This includes drugs to lower blood pressure and to reduce cholesterol. So we really are becoming a nation of pill takers but – and this is the point that I want to emphasize – we are not attacking the underlying causes of heart disease. One major cause of heart disease is physical inactivity. And, in the UK, we are becoming more inactive; we are taking less physical exercise. If you have a look at the statistics on your handout, you will see that these illustrate that since the 1970s the average number of

miles travelled on foot has dropped by around a quarter, just about 23%, and the number of miles travelled by bike has dropped by one-third. In other words, we are walking less, we are cycling less. By contrast, the number of miles people drive has increased by 70% over the same period of time. So, more use of the car and less physical exercise is the overall picture.

Add to this inactivity an unhealthy diet and the results are disastrous. Look at the figures for obesity in the UK. The percentage of obese adults has almost doubled in the last 12 years; a rise of about 92%. So, as a nation, we are becoming more obese as a result of poor diet and a lack of regular physical activity. And what does this mean in terms of life expectancy? Well, over 180,000 people die every year as a result of heart disease. And a third of these deaths – so, more than 60,000 deaths – according to the British Heart Foundation, are premature. In other words, people are dying earlier than they should do.

So, here in the UK we could do more. Other counties are already doing more. For instance, in the last ten years of the 20th century, Norway witnessed a drop of 54% in the number of deaths in men aged between 35 and 74. And, as we saw earlier in that same age group, Britain has a figure of 42%. So, although that seems good, we could and we should be doing more, and we should be looking at how to prevent heart disease rather than concentrating only on how to cure it.

CD1 Track 44
Ex 5.1

Listen and complete the sentences.

1. The government has introduced tax incentives to encourage investment in this region.
2. For tax purposes these organizations are often regarded as charities.
3. A number of reforms to the tax system have been proposed.

CD1 Track 45
Ex 5.2

Read the explanation below and listen to the examples.

add up

What are these?

the main objective

do anything

try out

no idea of it

next day

rapid growth

CD1 Track 46
Ex 5.3

Listen to the phrases. Mark the phrases with the symbols from Ex 5.2.

1. they invested in property
2. a mixture of oil and residues
3. it's an open market
4. it's due on Friday morning
5. free admission on Sundays
6. it shows as a white mark

CD1 Track 47
Ex 5.4

Listen and complete the text with two to five words in each space.

Real options

I'm going to go through the theory of real options, and then I'm going to show you how they can be used to raise some money, particularly on property assets. 'Real options' is a term which was coined ten or 15 years ago, when people began to realize that net present value isn't the only thing you should look at in valuing assets, that a number of assets in companies have a great deal of option value. And so the option theory you've been looking at can also be applied to real assets instead of just financial assets. And that, in raising money, companies particularly have a lot more to offer from an option pricing perspective than they first thought. The idea of real options is that management is not just a passive participant, but that management can take an active role in making and revising decisions that can lead on from unexpected market developments such as, for example, the price of oil has gone up from about $85 a barrel to in excess of $100 a barrel over the last year. So, if you were an oil producer this time last year, you would be taking a very different view on the market for oil. So the increase in oil prices has uncovered a stream of options which make oil producers a lot more valuable, and now you can bring oilfields back on stream that were not necessarily economic. So this is the kind of idea that when we're looking at a project, we're not just looking at a static cash flow, we're actually looking at a cash flow that can be subject to a lot of optionality.

Unit 6: Introducing new terminology

CD2 Track 1
Ex 2.1

Listen to the extract and make notes.

Embedded words

I've been doing some research on one particular problem that arises out of this, and I'd like to use that as a kind of a peg to hang this issue on, to tell you a little bit about it and where we've been getting with this. It's the problem sometimes called the problem of embedded words. So, when we hear a word of several syllables like *responsibility*, a word like *responsibility* invariably contains several smaller English words. So in the case of *responsibility*, we have – you can see here – *response*, *sponsor*, you have *ability* at the end there, and *bill* in the middle there and there's a few others, if you looked hard enough you'd find some more. But almost any word in the English language that has more than two syllables will invariably contain within it, packaged up inside it, smaller English words. Now, consider what the brain is faced with if somebody produces a sentence containing the word *responsibility*. And if the brain wrongly segments *responsibility* into *response* and *ability*, the decoding of that sentence is going to go catastrophically wrong. You see the point I'm making. So when we hear *responsibility*, it's that word; it's not a combination of *response* and *ability*.

CD2 Track 2
Ex 3.2

Listen to the extract and complete the table.

European Union regulations and directives

OK, so the two types of law I want to talk to you about today are directives and regulations, and these are very different, both in the way they are introduced and also in their scope, in the sense that one of them is more concerned with more serious matters while the other is more concerned with minor technical matters. Anyway, I'll return to this in a moment and give you more details and more examples, but before I do that, I want to remind you of some of the key players in the EU as far as law-making is concerned. You might remember – I hope you remember – that there is the European Commission, and the Council of

Ministers and the European Parliament, and all these have a role in law-making. The European Commission is a non-elected organization, which is responsible for the day-to-day running of the EU. You can think of it as a civil service, or the administrators if you like, also called the 'bureaucrats of Brussels', which is where the Commission is based. Then you have the Council of Ministers, which consists of one minister from each of the member states, so these are ministers who are part of the government in their own countries. Do you remember this? Yes? No? But that's clear, yeah, it is? Good. And finally we have the European Parliament, which consists of members who are elected in their own countries to work as full-time MEPs, that is Members of the European Parliament.

So, what roles do these organizations play in law-making and what is the difference between regulations and directives?

Well, first, regulations. So, regulations come either directly from the Commission or from the Council of Ministers and they tend to be concerned with pretty minor technical matters, for example, how much beef there needs to be in a beef sausage, for example or, how much real cream there has to be in ice cream. But they are not all trivial and unimportant things. There are regulations about standards of security in EU passports, for example.

And these regulations come into force as soon as they are published in what is called the *Official Journal*. So in other words, on the same day that these regulations are published, people in all the member states have to observe them, unless, and this is very important, unless individual member states have opted out of that particular area covered by the regulation. Yeah? Let me give you an example of what I mean by opting out. Both the UK and Ireland decided that they wanted to keep control of the whole area of visas and political asylum so they opted out. They said we will not be covered by EU regulation about those issues, yeah so that's fine. So that's regulations. Now what about directives? Well, there are two main differences. The first is that directives have to be accepted first by the Council of Ministers. The Commission cannot do this on its own and the European Parliament cannot do this on its own. Directives can only come from the Council of Ministers. And even then the directive does not become legally binding in any member state until the parliament of that state introduces domestic laws to give the directive effect. So, for

example, the directive comes from the Council of Europe, but it does not automatically become law in Britain, for example. It is only legally binding, it only has legal effect, when the British parliament passes a British law. So it is not the case that we are governed by European laws – many people believe that to be the case, but it is simply not true. There have to be British laws. Is that clear? I know it's a bit complex.

CD2 Track 3
Ex 4.3

Listen to the extract and make notes on the lecturer's definitions of both terms.

Market dominance and monopoly
What do I mean by making the distinction between market dominance and monopoly? We all know what a monopoly is, don't we? It's a single-firm case where the firm is in sole control of a market, and it's protected by such high entry barriers that its position is not vulnerable to competition. It's very rare in the real world for such firms to be in that happy position of being a complete monopoly. In the real world, however, you very often find that you have an approximation to dominance. Now, I've got an example … just looking for a single piece of paper. Oh, here we are. I undertook a study in the mid-'80s and it was quite easy for me to find 22 markets. The period covered, by the way, was mid-'70s to mid-'80s. It was quite easy to find a number of markets where the first firm had a share of 50% or above. In some cases much higher; closer to sort of 80 or 90% even. And the second-largest firm, or firms, were only half or less of the size, in terms of market share, of the dominant firm. So, although in many cases in the real world, you don't have monopoly – you only find that usually in the case of natural monopoly – the notion of dominance, as I want to use it, is quite frequent. You do frequently find one firm with a very sizeable market share – as a rule of thumb, if you like, upwards of 50%, sometimes even as high as 80 or 90%. And the second-largest firm, or firms, has a share perhaps under 10%, or a number of smaller firms all of whom have quite small market shares. Now, I therefore mean by dominance that sort of market structure. The size distribution of firms is highly skewed. You've got one firm in pretty much command of the market but a number of other firms operating in the market in competition.

CD2 Track 4

Ex 5.1

Listen to the following pairs of sentences. What is the difference in the pronunciation of the bold words in each pair?

1. a. What time **does** the train leave?
   b. I'm not sure why he's late. He **does** know about the meeting.

2. a. **Some** researchers have taken a different approach.
   b. We've just got time for **some** questions.

3. a. It was heated to 150°C **for** ten minutes.
   b. There are arguments **for** and against GM crop trials.

4. a. I'm not sure what you're getting **at**.
   b. There were **at** least five errors in the programme.

5. a. Increasingly, small memory devices **can** store large amounts of data.
   b. Well, I **can** do it, but I don't want to.

6. a. Oh, are they going to interview **us** as well as the students?
   b. Can you tell **us** what you've found?

CD2 Track 5

Ex 5.3

Listen and complete the extract with three to five words in each space. In each case, at least one of the missing words is a function word.

Multiple-choice questions – dead easy. They reduce interviewer bias; very easy for people to … very easy and fast for people to answer; very easy for data processing. But the argument goes that they are rather difficult to design. The thing about multiple-choice questions is that you are forcing people into certain answers. This is a good reason for piloting. If you have a multiple-choice question and you pilot it, you may find that people are not, they don't put the issue that you're asking them into that particular set of categories that you've imposed. So that's where your pilots and qualitative research will help. Let me just show you an example of this.

Unit 7: What lecturers do in lectures

CD2 Track 6

Ex 2.2

The lecturer talks about four methods of market research in this lecture. Listen and complete the list of methods that she mentions.

Doing market research

These are the four sort of most common ways, not necessarily in order, but if you're thinking of how market researchers collect their information, those are the ways they do it. Computers are being used to support market researchers a great deal more and the whole business of both selling things over the telephone and doing market research over the telephone has become a very important issue in market research and you'll see reference to terms like CATI: computer-assisted telephone interviewing. I think it probably goes without saying now that when you're phoned up and somebody wants to conduct a market research interview with you, they're probably sitting in front of a PC and we'll look at some of the implications of that. But one of the main ones, of course, is that the data entry occurs at the same time as the asking of the questions, so there's huge savings in terms of that and indeed some of the analysis can go on more or less as you're speaking; things like, you know, in questionnaires you'll need to skip from one section to another, well the computer does that automatically. Next week you're going to hear about a technique called 'adaptive conjoint analysis' and this is an analysis method that, as it suggests, sort of adapts to the person who's being interviewed and starts to react or ask different questions depending on the person.

Telephone interviewing is increasing in its coverage, its importance, but in some ways it's postal questionnaires that we want to concentrate on today, because it's postal questionnaires that in a sense have to be the most accurate, because postal questionnaires are the ones where the respondent doesn't have any help at all. There may be follow-ups and you may follow up by telephone and so on, but it's postal questionnaires which need to be the most accurate, if you like.

Personal interviewing in some ways is very good; very high levels of response, because – although you might have told somebody on the street who is trying to hassle you to answer a few questions to go away – the response rate for personal interviews is actually far higher than these other methods. People find it a lot more difficult to turn away somebody who's sort of standing there in front of them. The problem with personal interviews, of course, is that the interviewer is there and the interviewer themselves can bias the results, and I think it's a lesson in research in general that interviewer bias, of course, is to be avoided, but if you've got somebody in person and they say 'Well how about …?' or 'Do you mean …?' and this kind of thing and this is where distortions can come in. So, personal interviews are good – high response rates – but there is the problem of bias and of course they're very expensive, you're employing real people to ask these questions.

Telephone interviewing: less expensive, but a less good response rate and again some problems of bias. There's a problem whenever you're a person who's asking another person questions. There's always a problem of bias because you want people to expand on their answers and you want people to sort of chat about what they're interested in and therefore you have to interact with them and that interaction is what can cause the biases. The alternative is to have a very strict interviewing schedule and a very strict questionnaire, and you do get this particularly on the telephone where, you know, you get this sort of automaton who's actually a person but they're … it's a very stilted kind of interview and some would say that the quality of the data that is collected as a result is not that high. So we're concentrating on postal questionnaires but accepting that you need a good data collection device.

CD2 Track 7
Ex 3.2

Listen to Part 1 of the extract describing how the experiments were carried out. Complete the notes.

Social learning
Part 1

So it seems very plausible that monkeys in the wild learn to fear snakes from other monkeys who've already acquired the fear. And Mineka set up an experimental situation where observer monkeys could watch – who were, of course, naïve and didn't fear snakes initially, as you'll see – could watch a demonstrator who previously had learnt fear of snakes, for example, a wild-caught monkey. And the question is: what would the observers learn from the demonstrator? To explain the procedure before I show you the data, the observers were tested three times. First of all a pre-test when they were still naïve and they'd never seen a demonstrator acting afraid of snakes; a post-test immediately after they'd seen a demonstrator acting afraid of snakes; and then a follow-up three months later, with no intervening training, to see whether whatever they'd learnt was persistent. And the way the observers were tested was in a 'choice circus', which was just a round arena with four objects at the four corners, one of which was a model snake, and the other three were neutral objects, and they simply measured how much time the observer monkey would spend near the snake. If they were not frightened of snakes they'd spend about quarter of the time near the snake and a quarter of the time near the other objects. If they were afraid of the snake, they'd spend very little time near the snake and much, much more time near the other objects. So, how much time they spend near the snake is one measure of fear. The other measure of fear is that they used something called a 'Wisconsin test apparatus', which is an apparatus simply where monkeys have to reach over a gap to get food, and if you put a frightening stimulus in a glass box in the gap, the monkeys will be reluctant to reach over it to get to the food. So in this test they put either a real snake or a toy snake in a glass box and looked to see how slow the observers were to reach over the snake to get a tempting bit of food. And the slower they were and the more disturbed their behaviour, the more frightened they were concluded to be of snakes. So the question is: how did the observers' behaviour change as a function of watching the demonstrators?

CD2 Track 8
Ex 3.4

Listen to Part 2 of the extract. Make notes on the results and the conclusion the speaker draws from the results.

Part 2

What do the observers do? OK, here they are on the pre-test when they're not afraid of snakes at all, and as you can see they divide their time equally between the four stimuli. They show no avoidance of snakes at all at the pre-test. But at the post-test – when they've had an opportunity to watch an observer who is in the presence of a snake and acting frightened – now they behave not as frightened as the demonstrator monkey, but very much more like the demonstrator. They spend a lot of time near the neutral stimulus and very little time near the snakes. So they have acquired a fear of snakes just by watching another monkey. And this fear is just as strong at the three-month follow-up as it was immediately after. So this is evidence that naïve rhesus monkeys who are not afraid of snakes to start off can learn that snakes are dangerous just by watching another monkey. They don't have to be bitten by a snake or attacked by a snake or anything, they can just learn by watching another monkey.

CD2 Track 9
Ex 4.2

Listen to the extract and complete the notes.

Contestable markets

Essentially, what the theory predicts is that if an incumbent firm in such a market tries to raise its price above the marginal cost, an entrant can immediately appear, undercut that price so long as it's in excess of the marginal cost, and still make a profit. So, if the incumbent firm responds and drops its own price to marginal cost, then the new firm, having made a profit previously, can then leave costlessly. The knowledge on the part of the incumbent firm that that is the case – that if it tries to raise its price, or if there are two or three incumbent firms if they try to raise their price, it would immediately provoke entry and the price will then sink to marginal cost – will mean that the incumbent firms will be unable to raise their price above marginal cost. The significance therefore of the notion of perfectly free entry and exit, you can see – well, I hope – it's significant that here was a theory which was saying even if you've got very highly concentrated oligopolies, if these conditions hold, then you needn't worry; there are very, very few policies you need to adopt towards such industries because they will produce a performance which is in line with that of a perfectly competitive market.

My critique, or the critique of others as well, about the theory of perfect contestability is that if you change the assumptions slightly, the predictions change dramatically. It's very unstable. Let me give you an example of how … of what I mean by that. If in a particular market, for example, which a number of people

have said is contestable, if there are inevitable delays between a firm announcing it's coming into the market and actually managing to produce – and if in coming into the market the entrant has to incur some sunk costs – they can only be slight sunk costs. So if there's a delay, a slight delay, between the firm saying 'I will come into the market', the firm has to build up capacity, there's a delay between the announcement and the actual production, and also if there are some slight exit costs – sunk costs – that the firm has to incur to come into the market, then the predictions of the model are dramatically different. An incumbent firm in such a market can charge the monopoly price, or if it's two or three firms they can charge near the monopoly price. They can charge near the monopoly price until the entrant appears. They can then immediately drop their price to the marginal cost. The entrant, having finally come into production, would then make no money, in fact it would make a loss, it would make a loss equal to its sunk costs. If the entrant is aware of that, it would not come into the market. So the sequence is this, that, with slight alterations, if the notion of a perfectly contestable market is not met, if you make slight changes to the assumptions, even though the market may be approximately contestable, it may make a dramatic difference in the prediction because it means that the incumbent firms will continually be able to charge something approaching a monopoly price. Entry will not occur because the entrants will say, 'I have to incur some slight sunk costs to get into this market, and I won't be able to recover them, and I won't make any money because as soon as I appear and produce, the price will collapse to the marginal cost.'

CD2 Track 10
Ex 5.2

Listen to the following short lecture extracts.

1. Earthquakes are a relatively rare occurrence in the United Kingdom, and when they do occur, they are generally of such low magnitude that they are frequently not recognized as such.

2. Although hospital workers may be exposed to fairly low levels of radiation, measures need to be taken to keep exposure to a minimum.

3. Japan emerged from the postwar period with a developed electronics industry, and its emergence on the global consumer

goods market gave European manufacturers strong competition.

4. It is widely assumed that poverty exists only in developing countries, but this assumption has meant the needs of the urban poor in developed countries are often neglected.

5. The particles collide at something near the speed of light and this collision releases massive amounts of energy.

6. A lot of time was spent trying to involve parents in the road safety scheme, because previous experience has shown that the involvement of the local community in such projects is essential to their success.

7. Research has shown that male lions in different parts of Africa behave in different ways when faced with danger. Do environmental factors account for these differences in behaviour?

8. We studied the performance of these financial products over a period of three years, and we found that some perform significantly better than others.

CD2 Track 11
Ex 5.3

Listen to the following short texts and complete them with words or phrases that are synonyms.

1. Many people are worried that young people lack strong role models, and this concern has prompted the police to question the conduct of professional footballers, whose actions may have a significant influence on young men.

2. The USA decided to stay away from the Moscow Olympics in 1980, in protest at the Soviet Union's invasion of Afghanistan. Four years later, the Soviet Union retaliated with its own boycott of the Los Angeles Olympics.

3. Many multinational companies prefer to team up with local enterprises. Such alliances have a number of advantages.

4. The public's perception of the government's handling of the economy was critical. While the economy had in fact grown by 2%, people viewed the high unemployment rate and the government's inability to control strikes as indicators of poor performance.

Unit 8: Digressions

CD2 Track 12
Ex 2.2

Listen and read the extract. Then answer the questions.

My first set of examples come from a – and I'm going to talk about some fairly classic experiments in this lecture, but I would point out before I go on that there is a really excellent chapter on this subject in Shettleworth's book, which is referred to in the reference list for this lecture. Sara Shettleworth has a superb chapter on social learning. It's called 'Learning from others'. It's very up-to-date, very thoughtful, very comprehensive, and I'm just going to mention just a few of the examples that she mentions. But if you seriously want to think about this area, and it involves many complexities, her chapter is a very good place to go. Anyway, some of the best-known work on social learning, or putative social learning, in rats, in animals, are about food preferences. These are examples of learning the significance of stimuli, learning what foods are good to eat and what foods are bad to eat.

CD2 Track 13
Ex 3.1

Listen to Part 1 and make notes on the main points of the lecture.

Questionnaire design
Part 1

Now, I'm going to show you lots of examples of different types of questions that you can ask, and here are some very general design issues, though. Your questions, they need to be precise, as you'll see in a moment. They need to be well-ordered. Incidentally – sorry, I should have mentioned this earlier – the assessment for this course will, I think, be announced next week, formally, but what it's going to be is a case study. Basically you're going to be asked to evaluate, to comment, appraise. And it'll be a case study describing a, sort of, typical market research process, but it will also include data. There will be data that you can analyze to support your case, and you will be able to analyze it, basically, in whatever way that you want. That'll be up to you. Somebody was asking earlier about will we have to do a questionnaire, and they've probably been talking to people last year who did it and where everybody – basically every single individual –

ran a questionnaire and it basically just got out of hand. It was extremely difficult to mark because people were producing huge volumes of stuff. But this session now is just basically to introduce you to how this sort of data is collected, but you won't be doing this as part of the assessment. So, your questions, they need to be precise, and I'm going to show you some examples of good and bad questions in a moment. You need to decide very carefully, I think, on the ordering. I think there's really not an excuse for it these days, in a sense, for getting this part of it wrong and certainly presentation is very important so we'll talk a little bit about presentation and how you're able to order your questions to make sure that you get – well, there's different schools of thought, but – to make sure that you get optimum response.

CD2 Track 14
Ex 4.2

Listen to Part 2 and answer the questions. Then compare your answers with your group.

Part 2

So you've got to set very clear objectives as to what your questionnaire is designed to achieve. You need to say something about how you're going to collect the data, the sorts of question that you're going to have, the way that you word them, the flow of the questionnaire and so on. Obtaining approval is very important. In the university we have a body known as the Ethics Committee. Technically speaking, if you go out, well if you go outside the university to research anything, you need to get the approval of the Ethics Committee. And the Ethics Committee is, in many ways, a very good idea. The university, and indeed any market research body, that doesn't want its name pulled down by the market research process, of course, so we have to, if we're going out and indeed if students are doing projects, we have to get the implicit approval of the Ethics Committee. Sometimes that can come from the head of the department.

But two or three years ago, just for your information, the group, this group was actually a group of undergraduate students, they decided to do a market research project which was part of the assessment for the course. And they were given a free choice as to what subject they wanted to ask people about. And the explicit instruction was that the people they researched should only be members of the course. And this group came and said 'we

want to do a kind of a sex survey'. And what this was, it was actually fairly innocent, although I did say, you know, this must be kept strictly within the group, and it, sort of, well, I won't go into the details, but it was asking various pretty personal questions really. And the next thing I heard, the next thing I heard of it, was somebody called up from – I can't remember where – but they'd actually been accosted by one of these students somewhere downtown and been asked these questions. And as you can imagine we got into a little bit of trouble about it, and we hadn't cleared it, I hadn't cleared it basically with the committee, because it wasn't, well, I didn't believe it was going out – I didn't think it was going outside. So, anyway, there are, obviously very potential problems in that, but you do need to obtain approval. There is a Market Research Society code of practice on asking questions, on how to do research.

You need to pre-test the questionnaire. This is really important. Those of you, some of you, will be doing this for, you know, your dissertation. Some of you, I know, are collecting primary data. You need to pre-test the thing, because you're the researcher. You're very close to the subject. You know what you're talking about. But you've got to check that other people do as well. And if you want a statistically valid sample of a hundred or two hundred people, then you've got to make sure that you're collecting the data properly. And it's here that these pre-tests, or pilots, they're going to tell you whether it's going to work or not.

So make sure that you do pilots and, you know, this can be, sort of, half a dozen different people that you question. I mean you'll soon find out whether you've got any potential … or any doubts about the length of the questionnaire or the style of particular questions, or whether the sort of questions that you're asking are valid. You'll soon find out from that. So, piloting or pre-testing is really important.

CD2 Track 15
Ex 5.2

Listen to the extract. Which of the activities in 5.1 did the lecturer mention?
Now here's an idea out of the 70s, IRD – integrated rural development. This was the idea that when you worked in rural areas with the poor, and the smallholder and so on, what you tried to do was deliver a package of assistance across the sectors, on the grounds this would give you synergy.

Now just to give you a fairly exaggerated example, if you're trying to get people to plant new varieties of rice and use fertilizer to increase their yields, which you hope is a scale-neutral technology that can be used by smallholders, then why not at the same time combat malaria, inoculate people against disease, clean up the water supply? Because all of these will give you better health, which is a good thing in itself but, of course, healthier farmers can work harder in the fields and so that complements the agricultural measures. And while we're at it, we're going to build some new access roads, because that will improve price relatives at the farm gate and reduce isolation. And while we're at it, we'll run an adult literacy campaign, because literate farmers can read the labels on fertiliser packs, and so on and so forth.

So there was the idea that you should try and do things in development in an integrated fashion across all sectors, because you get synergy, and you get more than the sum of the parts going on. Now integrated rural development was very, very exciting to work in. You got all kinds of things to have a go at, and you've got quite a lot of resources to play with, but these resources were limited compared with needs. So what happened with integrated rural development was within any country, what you did was you took a country, and a country might look just like that, and it might have its capital there, and you take a country that looks just like that, and you do integrated rural development and you do it there, there, there, there, there, oh and there. And yes, that is to scale yes, that is to scale. In other words, you get these little enclaves of very small areas, where donors are putting in resources and everything is done.

And in the early 1970s, Kenya had six small integrated rural programmes, which were very, very well documented and some contemporary, very influential thinkers about development worked on those projects in the early 1970s. But look how tiny they are. That really is to scale. These things were in very small areas indeed. Why? Because, although you could target resources for a small area, you couldn't have the whole country running the kind of programmes that were run there. So because you did everything in integrated rural development, you could only do it on a small scale, concentrated in particular areas.

Now those six small experiences, I think, were all successes. They were successes, but I think, with the benefit of hindsight, we would have to say that they were unrepeatable and institutionally unsustainable. When the donors got bored, and the funds ran out, and the foreign experts' contracts ended, and the Land Rovers began to rust, these projects essentially stopped. Indeed, I arrived in this part of Kenya in 1979, which had been the administrative headquarters, and there were two or three filing cabinets chock-a with files in my room. And I left them there for a while, and then one day I thought, what on earth? And I went through these filing cabinets, and it was sort of all the stuff on, sort of, four or five years, ten years earlier, of the implementation of this. Minutes, plans, documents, contracts, budgets, semi-annual reports, monthly reports, all this kind of stuff. And I looked at this, and I said, my goodness, this is a vital bit of development history here, but it's clogging up my office. So it all went in the skip. There's never, never enough historians around to document these experiences, and that's the sort of way. And as I threw them into the skip, I thought, well there you go, good idea at the time, good people working on it, quite a success, but not sustainable.

CD2 Track 16
Ex 6.1

Listen and complete the notes.

I think that realism excludes the possibility – and it's a growing one – that states can simply isolate themselves from the outside world. The growth of television, the growth of mass communications, have meant that it's virtually impossible for states to ignore what's going on around them, and public opinion has become more important in some respects within states, forcing states to do things that they might not otherwise do. So the strict application of power in terms of maintaining the hierarchy, of ignoring the interests of others, is simply slowly being withered away.

CD2 Track 17
Ex 6.3

Listen and complete the notes.

Ten years later, therefore, we have the Scandinavian ideas impacting on British office design. Another illustration of that might be, you'll discover in the course of the lecture, that some of the factors which are driving the unusual, sometimes, configuration of office buildings on the Continent, not always but sometimes, are to do with employment legislation – workers' councils, employers' rights, employees' rights.

CD2 Track 18
Ex 6.5

Listen and complete the notes.

Nineteen eighty-two. None of the commercial banks gave any money to the developing world for the best part of ten years after the '82 debt crisis. They got such a bad fright by the debt crisis they more or less ceased lending to the developing world. So the only people who were lending money to governments in the developing world from 1982 onwards were other governments, other aid agencies and other multilateral agencies like the IMF and the World Bank.

Software Licence for English for Academic Study: Listening DVD.

English for Academic Study

Other books in the best-selling *English for Academic Study* series

To succeed in their academic studies, students need excellent reading, writing, speaking and listening skills. The *English for Academic Study* series provides everything you need to prepare for English-medium academic study.

This series is based on work carried out on pre-sessional courses at the University of Reading's International Study and Language Institute. It is supported by authentic reading texts and lectures.

Course Books provide:

- topics and activities to challenge and stimulate students on pre-sessional and pre-departure university courses
- step-by-step activities supported by recent research into EAP methodology
- materials written by EAP professionals that reflect current developments in language teaching for academic purposes
- book maps for easy reference
- study tips in every unit
- full glossaries of terms
- weblinks with additional information and activities

A dedicated EAS website offers further teacher and student resources.

Teacher's Books are clearly structured, comprehensive and contain full answer keys and model answers.

Study Books are intended for self-study outside formal class time and include full answer keys.

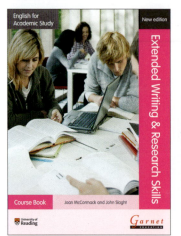

English for Academic Study — Extended Writing & Research Skills
New edition
Course Book — Joan McCormack and John Slaght
University of Reading / Garnet Education

Course Book with CDs:
ISBN: **978 1 90861 430 8**

Teacher's Book:
ISBN: **978 1 90861 431 5**

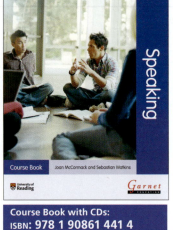

English for Academic Study — Speaking
New edition
Course Book — Joan McCormack and Sebastian Watkins
University of Reading / Garnet Education

Course Book with CDs:
ISBN: **978 1 90861 441 4**

Teacher's Book:
ISBN: **978 1 90861 442 1**

English for Academic Study — Writing
New edition
Course Book — Anne Pallant
University of Reading / Garnet Education

Course Book:
ISBN: **978 1 90861 439 1**

Teacher's Book:
ISBN: **978 1 90861 440 7**

Source Book:
ISBN: **978 1 90861 436 0**

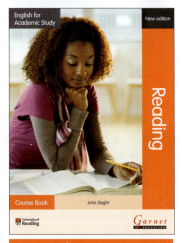

English for Academic Study — Reading
New edition
Course Book — John Slaght
University of Reading / Garnet Education

Course Book:
ISBN: **978 1 90861 437 7**

Teacher's Book:
ISBN: **978 1 90861 438 4**

Source Book:
ISBN: **978 1 90861 436 0**

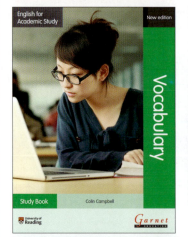

English for Academic Study — Vocabulary
New edition
Study Book — Colin Campbell
University of Reading / Garnet Education

Study Book:
ISBN: **978 1 90861 443 8**

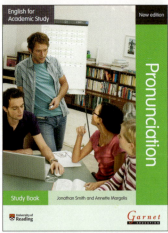

English for Academic Study — Pronunciation
New edition
Study Book — Jonathan Smith and Annette Margolis
University of Reading / Garnet Education

Study Book with CDs:
ISBN: **978 1 90861 435 3**